Democracy, the Market, and the Firm

Democracy, the Market, and the Firm

How the Interplay between Trading and Voting Fosters Political Stability and Economic Efficiency

HERVÉ CRÈS
MICH TVEDE

UNIVERSITY PRESS

Great Clarendon Street, Oxford, OX2 6DP,
United Kingdom

Oxford University Press is a department of the University of Oxford.
It furthers the University's objective of excellence in research, scholarship,
and education by publishing worldwide. Oxford is a registered trade mark of
Oxford University Press in the UK and in certain other countries

Published in the United States of America by Oxford University Press
198 Madison Avenue, New York, NY 10016, United States of America

British Library Cataloguing in Publication Data
Data available

Library of Congress Control Number: 2021935298

ISBN 978–0–19–289473–1

DOI: 10.1093/oso/9780192894731.001.0001

Printed and bound in the UK by
TJ Books Limited

Links to third party websites are provided by Oxford in good faith and
for information only. Oxford disclaims any responsibility for the materials
contained in any third party website referenced in this work.

Foreword

This book is an attempt to resolve an enigma that has puzzled social scientists since the works of Condorcet (1785): Why are collective choices *in practice* so stable and easy to make, when *in theory* it should be totally otherwise? A striking illustration of this enigma is the almost unanimous support of shareholders of publicly traded companies for the motions tabled by directors.

The book proposes two main arguments. The first one lies in the interplay between the voting and trading mechanisms. It explores how a symbiosis between voting and trading can attenuate the failures of both the market to promote economic efficiency and the majority principle to achieve political stability. Figuratively speaking, it argues that the invisible hand of the market and the raised hand of democracy work, hand in hand, to give rise to a more responsible world.

The second argument lies in the feedback from collective choices onto individual preferences. It explores the behavioral assumptions leading to an alignment of individual preferences.

The analysis relies on formal models which are kept as simple as possible, and which make use only of elementary convex and vector analysis.

We would like to thank Alessandro Citanna, Itzhak Gilboa, and especially the late and sorely missed Philippe Mongin for their comments on various drafts of the manuscript. We express our gratitude to Yves Balasko and Bruno Latour for so many inspiring conversations. We owe a special tribute to Mehdi Hamadi for collecting the data on CAC 40 General Assemblies, and to Myles O'Byrne for translating the text in English. Many thanks also to the Oxford University Press team, especially to Henry Clarke, Nicola Maclean, Kalpana Sagayanathan, and Adam Swallow, for their support during the editorial process. Hervé Crès gratefully acknowledges support from Tamkeen under the NYUAD Research Institute award for project CG005 and from the Center for Institutional Behavioral Design (C-BID).

Contents

List of Figures

Introduction

Democracy and the Market, Hand in Hand

If there is one realm in which the democratic process achieves percentages worthy of a dictator, it is the corporate world. One striking, if not altogether surprising, illustration of this is the General Assemblies (GAs) of the firms listed on the French CAC 40. Between 2011 and 2015, their boards of directors tabled a total of 3,861 motions to be voted on by shareholders.[1] It is noteworthy that on average these were carried with a majority of more than 94 percent. To give the reader a clear picture of the level of support for such proposals, consider the following consensus index: more than 86 percent of them were adopted with majorities larger than 86 percent. Why so much consensus?

The Invisible Hand of the Market

A hard-core neoclassical economist would be perfectly untroubled by this alignment between shareholders. Indeed, on the contrary, she would interpret it as proof that the markets are perfect, and her demonstration is an act of faith: shareholders are also consumers, and to improve their welfare they exchange goods and services in space and time in accordance with market prices as part of a process of optimization which ultimately sees them agree with the values associated with these prices. What is more, a magical and invisible hand ensures that prices adjust to balance supply and demand. This narrative ends with consumers all in agreement about the values represented by these equilibrium prices and therefore about the best way to manage the firms in which they hold shares: maximize profits and in turn their wealth and individual welfare. Seen in this light, not only does the invisible hand of the market eliminate the disparity between supply and demand, it also wipes out any disagreement between shareholders when taking collective decisions as the owners of a firm.

---

[1] This represents between 708 and 822 each year. See Appendix A for the comprehensive data.

Democracy, the Market, and the Firm: How the Interplay between Trading and Voting Fosters Political Stability and Economic Efficiency. Hervé Crès and Mich Tvede, Oxford University Press. © Hervé Crès and Mich Tvede 2021.
DOI: 10.1093/oso/9780192894731.003.0001

So it is no surprise to see such consensus among the shareholders of the firms listed on the CAC 40. And to top it off, the market promotes a social optimum insofar as there is no alternative to the equilibrium that improves the welfare of somebody without impairing the welfare of somebody else. These concepts are straightforward, the demonstration is clear-cut, and the results are powerful. What more can we ask for?

Another economist, also neoclassical albeit more tempered, may have a more circumspect response to this doctrine. For it is difficult to believe that the markets are perfect. First of all because the firms on the CAC 40 are behemoths whose industrial strategies have an impact across their entire sectors by producing direct external effects, of production or pollution, or indirect effects, due for example to their capacity to influence prices. With just a few exceptions (for example, trading permits for carbon or sulfur dioxide emissions) these externalities are not subject to market transactions, and so the invisible hand cannot completely fulfil its endeavor of eliminating conflict between shareholders: residual disagreements remain, particularly over the question of whether or not it is opportune to maximize profits.

The second reason to question the neoclassical doctrine is that it is difficult to see the financial markets as complete and enabling each individual to protect herself against every conceivable risk or contingency. There are possible future states of the world to which no wealth can be transferred and between which no transaction is possible. This incompleteness partly amputates the invisible hand of the market, leaving it unable to act with full capacity, and so absolute consensus between shareholders cannot be achieved: here, too, there will be residual disagreements between shareholders, not so much over whether it is opportune to maximize profits but rather over how they want profits to be calculated.

In both cases, whether in the presence of externalities or financial incompleteness, there can be no alignment between relative prices and relative values of shareholders, because some things simply have no price. The third reason to challenge the hard-core neoclassical doctrine relates to the information asymmetries between stakeholders that lead to market failures; the fourth relates to the ambiguity of risks, which makes any coincidence between the beliefs of shareholders, and in turn their complete alignment, illusory. The list goes on.

The debate between these two hypothetical economists is in fact less clear-cut than all that, even though it remains very much dualistic. The hard-core neoclassicist is aware of the market's imperfections, but she feels they detract little from its genius. And above all she sees any attempt to correct these imperfections as dangerously uncertain and somewhat arrogant. This is not only the interventionist hubris of an omnipotent State, the caricatural and callow faith of certain elites. No, what is also uncertain and arrogant are targeted public interventions, whose interference with the smooth running of market transactions no-one can predict. The market's genius lies in the multitude of its stakeholders, all profoundly driven by their individual interests, all with a keen knowledge of their immediate environment, avid opportunists whose individual daring, through the forces of the market, combines to form a powerful and fertile collective adventure. An average majority of 94 percent and a consensus index of 86 percent: these are the scores (out of 100) that can be attributed to the invisible hand. Can anyone top that?

The Raised Hand of Democracy

As for our more tempered neoclassicist, he does not dispute the genius of the invisible hand, he simply gives thought to its limits. These are manifested in residual disagreements between shareholders that linger after transactions have been completed. But in order to reach collective decisions, these disagreements must be eliminated in ways other than through transactions. And so a vote at the GA is the natural solution. The vote should be seen as a *complementary* mechanism with which to eliminate disagreements between shareholders. To extend the metaphor, the raised hands at these meetings are indispensable to attenuate the failures of the invisible hand of the market.

There are many different ways to take collective decisions. These vary according to context: a household, partnership, association, trade union, company or any kind of public authority, whether executive, legislative or judicial, etc. And a formal vote need not necessarily be held to reach the final decision, once the deliberations have been exhausted. But whatever the circumstances, when an alternative to the status quo is being evaluated, the political weight behind it is tested. In this regard, the vote is a stylized representation of many informal processes. One need simply look to personal experience to see what a natural reflex it is to hold a vote when an informal process fails to produce a satisfactory conclusion. This is because voting is intuitive, easy to understand and implement, difficult to manipulate, and a universal phenomenon.[2] The

---

[2] Not to mention the fact that majority voting is the only social choice function that is neutral, anonymous and positively responsive (monotonous) in binary comparisons, as demonstrated by May (1952).

irony is that choosing a dictator is the only system that can compete with the voting process in such respects.

Yet, in light of what social choice theory teaches us, there is something mysterious about scores as high as 94 percent and 86 percent. There is nothing in what economists understand about how the majority vote works that can explain such astronomical percentages. Since Condorcet (1785), we have known that even minor disagreements between voters can bring about chaotic collective behavior (Black, 1958; McKelvey, 1976). And in the context being considered here, the slightest imperfection in the market should pave the way for disagreements between shareholders which, albeit residual, are nonetheless substantial, or in any case significant enough to make the near unanimity found in CAC 40 GAs difficult to explain.

This enigma is nothing new. It was met with surprise by Tullock (1981), a highly astute observer of the political world who asked: Why so much stability? For in the real world there is anything but chaos, "acts are passed with reasonable dispatch and then remain unchanged for very long periods" (p. 189). Tullock goes on: "theory and reality seem to be not only out of contact, but actually in sharp conflict."

The considerations facing any theorist wishing to evaluate the comparative merits of the market and the voting system when it comes to the allocation of resources are highly contrasted. The act of faith of the hard-core neoclassicist expresses an unequivocal and triumphant doctrine, while the faith of her more tempered colleague is imbued with doubt and pessimism. On the one hand, the theory of general equilibrium shored up by an abundance of existence theorems, in addition to two welfare theorems celebrating the miraculous concomitance of efficiency and equilibrium, of what is desirable and what occurs; on the other, social choice theory strewn by theorems of impossibility, inexistence and inefficiency, with almost no hope of seeing any rationality emerge from the collective. On one side, a victor boasts of the success of commercial transactions, and in particular the elimination of conflicts, thus ridding economic matters of all political concerns; on the other, the defeated is stumped by the failure of majority voting, and in particular its presumed inefficiency, which rids political matters of any economic interest. Case closed?

Democracy and the Market, Hand in Hand

It's not that straightforward. While support for the motions tabled by boards of directors stands at an average of 94 percent, in some cases it hovers around

50 percent and a decision must be made. Not even our hard-core neoclassicist challenges the capacity of the GA voting process to give legitimacy to the small proportion of decisions that are disputed. Indeed, this legitimacy appears in most cases to benefit from near unanimity; legitimacy and unanimity are both factors of stability, stability in both management and strategic direction, and a stable economic environment is itself conducive to trade. This all points to the conclusion that the smooth running of shareholder democracy facilitates the success of the market.

And inversely? There are two arguments to suggest that the smooth running of the market facilitates that of shareholder democracy. First, market transactions, albeit incomplete or limited, partly resolve disagreements between shareholders, and in so doing give greater homogeneity to the opinions of the voting population, in turn facilitating the emergence of a shared will. Second, shareholders at a GA are a collective entity that is formed endogenously rather than by the chance circumstances of their birth. Shareholders choose a firm for the purposes of insurance and savings. They invest in it to the extent that it proposes a production plan they believe in, a plan that allows them to protect themselves against risks they fear and/or to save money using whichever method suits them. Shareholders therefore have shared beliefs and needs: they believe in certain future developments and they need insurance and savings. One might suggest that this self-selection of shareholders on the market also gives greater homogeneity to the opinions of the voting population. Perhaps this alignment of opinions, albeit partial, through market transactions, ahead of the GA voting process, holds part of the key to unlocking the mystery of the overwhelming scores obtained?

Let us imagine, and take for granted for the purposes of simplicity, that the better the market works, the better democracy works and vice versa. Where does that leave us? The majority vote enables clear decisions, that much is true, but does it encourage the efficient allocation of resources?

It is reasonable to hope so. We will show that in a democracy the average voter plays a central role as she is well positioned to hold the keys to power to the extent that if her opinion prevails it is difficult to reverse by a majority vote, or at least more difficult to reverse than a less central opinion. And in the corporate world, the average shareholder has the best incentive to promote economic efficiency. Pushing the argument somewhat to make it clearer, all it takes for the majority vote to be efficient is a governance where the average voter and the average shareholder coincide.

Figuratively speaking, in the interaction between the trading and voting mechanisms, there is a gravitational force that tends towards the alignment of political power and economic efficiency. The two do not always coincide, far from it, in the same way that few falls are ever truly vertical, but this force is present nonetheless, and pulls in the right direction.

The Social Shareholder

However, this force is not in itself sufficient. As we will see, even if democracy and the market were a match made in heaven which we just allowed ourselves to imagine, they could never generate the near unanimity observed in the GAs of the CAC 40—unless one believes in the perfection of the market. On an imperfect market, the combined interplay of trading and voting may be harmonious, and potentially efficient, but not to the extent that it can explain the complete alignment between shareholders. At best one can expect to observe, as in modern democracy, the emergence of a left–right axis along which oppositions form, and more frequent alternation between the two at the level of senior management.

In the face of this enigma, the hard-core neoclassicist sticks to her guns. She asserts that markets do not fail as much as one thinks. In a glimmer of doubt, she may concede that economic models have some of the limitations identified, but will quickly recover by pointing out that everything happens as if the market were perfect, so why all this doubt?

As for her more tempered colleague, he wants to fully explore that doubt. He is caught between a rock and a hard place: the tempting comfort of orthodoxy and tradition, and the destructive heterodoxy repeatedly avowing that all such formalism must be dispensed with. He is solicited by dissidents from both sides outlining a range of hypotheses with which to resolve the enigma: shareholders have limited rationality; they defer to the board of directors, etc. OK, perhaps. Why not? But still … which limits in the rationality of shareholders are we talking about? And if shareholders defer to board members, why bother showing up to vote in the first place? And what about institutional investors? Do they defer to the board members? And so on. The tempered neoclassicist has no doubt that there are several plausible explanations, but is looking for one that is compatible with the neoclassical perspective and will survive any test of the resistance of general equilibrium.

So if the alignment of shareholders cannot be achieved in the marketplace, at the GA, or at the junction between the two, then it is achieved in a third space, or rather at the meeting point between these two spaces and a third. And the only space which we have not yet explored is the inner space of each shareholder. How do they reach their decisions? By optimizing, maybe, but how does the firm's political environment resonate in this optimization process? Are shareholders unwavering, rigidly sticking to their preferences, or do they adapt them over time to a changing environment and under the influence of collective decisions?

Simply raising this question is in itself a response. Humans are social animals imbued with a sense of the epoch in which they live. They adhere to different groups and share resources and information, as well as opinions, with their fellow humans. When an agent freely decides to invest in a firm, when she joins a group of shareholders, shows up to vote at the GA, etc., she displays an appetite for joint action—what the French legal tradition refers to as 'affectio societatis' and Hirschman (1970) names 'loyalty'. This willingness makes her susceptible to the opinions of the group, not so much those of its individual members but rather the wisdom of their collective deliberations, or the force which the decision-making protocol generates. Such wisdom and force cannot leave her indifferent. Let us be clear: one does not invest in the capital of a firm as one enters politics or joins the army, where body and soul are given over to the united cause, but one nonetheless opens up to the beliefs and tastes of others, subscribing to a shared destiny; the alternative is to defect ('exit' in Hirschman's words) and sell one's shares, or stay home, take the money and run...

Single Thought

In short, individuals shape the groups they join *and at the same time are shaped by them*. This duality between individuals and groups opens up new perspectives. The dynamic through which opinions are formed becomes circular: collective decisions reflect individual opinions, and individual opinions reciprocally evolve in light of collective decisions. This dynamic could become too self-referential: if individual opinions are framed by deliberations and collective judgments, given that these are determined by individual opinions in the first place, the serpent can be seen to eat its own tail, and ultimately all of the stakeholders converge towards a shared perspective; this is what is understood by single thought.[3]

---

[3] A reference to the French term *pensée unique*, developed in the 1990s by Jean-François Kahn to critique what he perceived as tendencies towards conformism or ideological domination. See Kahn (1995).

An in-depth study of this dynamic reveals one of the keys to shareholders' alignment. It relates to the shareholders' propensity to change their mind when subjected to the most extreme social pressure, when all of the GAs they attend, without exception, express the same opinion. Let us imagine that, in that case, shareholders do not want to be at odds with the opinion of all GAs they attend—a behavioral assumption that is called the Pareto principle. Ultimately, then, the system's only stable states are those in which there is alignment between the shareholders within each firm. This solves the enigma of the overwhelming scores obtained at the CAC 40 GAs, and without having to subscribe to the notion of the perfect market.

Firms as Social Laboratories?

The underlying big question is whether or not there is an alliance between the democratic and liberal mindsets in order to promote harmony and performance in all aspects of the economic, social, and political life of the polis, as measured by the health, peace, and prosperity of its citizens. The democratic mindset is that which guides collective decisions, made centrally for the purposes of unified and legitimate action for the common good, provided each stakeholder can express herself freely, for example by participating in deliberations and/or voting. The liberal mindset is that which guides individual decisions, made away from the center and serving private interests in a locus of action that is both free and open. The economic, social, and political life of the polis is made up of an amalgam of individual and collective decisions, and the rhythm of civic life alternates between personal and collective choices.

This underlying question can be asked in many different ways, can be approached from several angles, and can generate responses that are as varied as they are numerous. This essay is underpinned by a vision of firms, which bring together communities of stakeholders to manage shared assets, as laboratories in which voting and trading interact: the majority vote which embodies the democratic mindset within a centralized collective decision-making mechanism; and the trade in goods and securities which embodies the liberal mindset within a decentralized individual decision-making mechanism. This vision is first and foremost based on realism. Put simply, consumers exchange goods and services, invest in firms and (in some cases) vote at GAs. Trading and voting, at least for individual investors, are most of the time sincere acts, detached from all strategic considerations, exempt from ideological distortions, and sheltered from media manipulation. By focusing on the laboratory, what is lost in depth is gained in simplicity and precision. The decision to adopt this vision is also driven by certain limitations: it would be insurmountably difficult to conduct a more direct analysis of this underlying big question, especially if its conclusions were to retain the potency and sobriety of a theorem (as the authors would wish).

The alignment between shareholders at the CAC 40 GAs may seem anecdotal and relatively unsurprising, but its scale and systematic nature are striking. We are talking about thousands of individuals and about issues of importance in their lives. This alignment is easy to measure and is obtained frequently and in accordance with due process. Lastly, it relates to objective choices, most of which are measurable and are met by shareholders with a shared understanding. In short, it has all the features of a textbook scenario and brings us back to Tullock's surprise: Why so much consensus? This alignment is represented in Chapter 4 by Theorem 4.1, the 'single thought theorem'. It is left to the reader to decide to what extent this result defines the notion of single thought, reflects its intuition, and breaks down its mechanics. As for the authors' view, the reader is directed to the conclusion.

Summary of the Essay

This essay is divided into two parts. The first one outlines a vision of the political economy of the (publicly traded) firm, the second a vision of the social economics of shareholders. The dominant paradigm used by economists is to explain collective phenomena as the result of individual actions and of their mutual interactions—methodological individualism. The first part of this essay fully complies with this paradigm. The second part slightly enlarges it by considering how collective phenomena influence individual actions.

The first part of the essay is subdivided into three chapters. The first two add certain nuances to the dualistic view of an efficient market and an impossible social choice. Chapter 3 reveals the extent to which the combined interplay of trading and voting tends to level out the disputes between shareholders and facilitate efficient decisions. The content of this first part borrows from classical political and economic theory: the first chapter offers a *general equilibrium* model of trade in various contexts of market failures; the second chapter imports from *social choice theory* the tools and results that underpin the study of majority voting; the third chapter merges the two approaches and proposes an analysis of *social choice in general equilibrium* to resolve the opening puzzle of this essay: 'Why so much consensus?' The first part concludes with a statement of the limits of the classical approach, and leads into the second part, which includes elements borrowed from sociology and philosophy.

The second part of the essay is subdivided into two chapters. Chapter 4 incorporates the individual into a social network of shareholders, suggesting that a principle of reciprocal influence is at work between individuals and the groups to which they belong (the Pareto principle), and analyzes the circumstances that can lead to alignment between shareholders. Chapter 5 penetrates to the heart of the individual in an effort to sound out the root determinants of individual preferences, and endeavors to identify the intimate motives underlying the Pareto principle.

The content of the second part falls in line with that of the first part, but enriches the analysis with notions that first proved fruitful outside of classical political and economic thinking. Chapter 4 blurs the distinction between individuals and collectives, and underlines the *duality* of these two types of agents: individuals shape the collectives to which they belong, and at the same time they are shaped in return by these collectives—this duality is a classical consideration in sociology (Simmel, 1955). Chapter 5 focuses on the founding hypothesis of *stability of individual preferences*. It reviews recent efforts by economists to unlock this hypothesis and mobilizes some notions of the Stoic tradition. These openings toward duality and stoicism are by no means an attempt to subvert the classical approach; at most they are a useful, and in any case fertile, transgression.

PART I

THE POLITICAL ECONOMY
OF THE FIRM

Economic thought never unleashes as much power as when discussing *Homo economicus*. At its core is methodological individualism. This becomes clear when one considers how rich in possibilities and refinement the theory of individual decision-making is, how agency theory has given us a better understanding of human organizations, and how game theory has branched off into the social sciences.[1]

As we will see in Chapter 2, economic thought is less triumphant when representing collective action. It runs up against walls of impossibility, gets bogged down in paradoxes, and strays off haphazardly along paths that lead everywhere and therefore nowhere.[2] Efforts to model the choices made in firms suffer from this: that which is essential is overlooked or short-circuited.

An All-Too-Human Black Box

General equilibrium theorists (e.g. Balasko, 1988, 2011; Mas-Colell, 1985) have deployed remarkable inventiveness to model the technical aspects of production, understand the decisions reached by economic engineers, and explain the root impetus of value creation. But they confine the 'rationality' of the choices made by firms to one catch-all concept: the *objective function* which must be optimized. The most common objective is profit. No surprise, given that since Fisher's separation theorem (1930) we have known that on a perfect market this objective is unanimously pursued by shareholders regardless of their preferences. But we also know that this is not the case on an imperfect

[1] See Gilboa (2009); Laffont & Martimort (2002); and Dixit & Nalebuff (1993) respectively.
[2] See Arrow (1951); Condorcet (1785); Kornhauser & Sager (1986); and McKelvey (1976) respectively.

market. No matter, if not profit then the objective will be the 'real wealth' or the 'shareholders' wealth', etc.[3] But whatever the objective to be optimized, the firm is seen as a black box with anthropomorphic contours.

Industrial organization theorists (e.g. Tirole, 1988) have explored other aspects of the problem: strategic stakes, market structure, or competition regulations (or lack thereof), in most cases adopting a partial-equilibrium approach. But here, too, the firm is seen as an agent that is virtually indistinguishable from *Homo economicus*: it is considered to have individual rationality and described as serving an objective, with hardly any effort to describe the political mechanism that leads to this function other than to say that a leader is appointed who acts on behalf of the legal entity.[4] Only agency theorists have departed from this monolithic vision of firms, exploring individual decisions *within* firms, the different possible legal statuses, and contract engineering. But their focus is rarely decision-making in a social, political or market context, and remains confined within the firm's walls and concentrated on the art of management.

This rigid view of firms can be traced back to the work of the classicists, who focused on the individual entrepreneur. At best it is more normative than positive. It involves identifying what firms should decide rather than understanding what they do decide. At worst it props up our anthropocentric bias in interpreting collective actions, our tendency to imagine that there is a *reason* and a *will* behind each political phenomenon—a tendency which, when caricatured, is known as conspiracy theory.

Dehumanizing the Firm

We can sense that there is a need for a less naive approach to firms, one in which production-related decisions are not necessarily based on a rationality which mimics that of individuals. Organization theory is replete with representations of firms that depart from the rational choice paradigm. Morgan (2006) describes representations inspired by machines, organisms, brains, cultures, and political systems.[5] Crès, et al. (2013) propose a bureaucratic

---

[3] See Dierker & Grodal (1999) and Bejan (2008) respectively. See also Gabszewicz & Vial (1972).

[4] This view can be seen to reflect Arrow's impossibility theorem: firms can only survive on the market in the long term if they are rational; the only proper way to do this, i.e. which satisfies the principles of unanimity and independence, is to choose a dictator, even though this reasoning is clearly somewhat tenuous.

[5] Machines (Taylor, 1911; Fayol, 1919; Weber, 1924); organisms (Parsons, 1951; Burns & Stalker, 1961); brains (Sandelands & Stablein, 1987; Walsh & Ungson, 1991; March, 1999); cultures (Ouchi & Wilkins, 1985); political systems (Burns, 1961; March, 1962).

organizational model determined only by feasibility constraints and free of any objective.[6]

In this essay, the rational choice paradigm is eschewed in relation to firms, as is any notion of limited rationality: firms have no reason, no will, and no objective function. All they have are management and governance bodies. And what we observe in firms is that decisions are made at board meetings and subsequently validated at the GA. Our purpose here is to characterize politically stable decisions, those which by definition are most likely to prevail in the long term, and are therefore the only ones capable of constituting regularities. Such regularities are the result of the interplay of forces at work within the firm, in accordance with the procedures set out by its governance structure and in line with a protocol which at times can appear somewhat mechanical. The challenge is to model the *aggregation mechanism* through which these forces combine, to open up the black box of the firm in a context of general equilibrium.

In response to such a challenge, the economist's natural reflex is to model what happens in the firm as the interplay between various individual stakeholders with objective functions.[7] The political scientist's natural reflex is to consider the balance of power both within and outside the firm, between all of its stakeholders, without overlooking the importance of symbols and allowing more room for subjectivity.[8] At the intersection of these two approaches, in the purest tradition of political economy, one finds those models in which the interplay is simply a vote and the balance of power is determined at the ballot box;[9] and it is in this vein that the political economy of the firm is laid out in the pages that follow. It is rooted in the agreements and disagreements generated by market exchanges (Chapter 1). At its core is the (in)stability of the resulting political configurations with regard to the majority principle (Chapter 2). And the fruit it bears is the symbiosis between individual and collective choices in our economies, the lasting and mutually beneficial relationship between the voting and trading mechanisms (Chapter 3).

---

[6] The complexity of the problems to solve is such that organizations are forced to rely on solutions found in the past, in a case-based approach to decision-making (Gilboa & Schmeidler, 1995). This produced a finding evocative of Arrow's theorem: feasibility can only be assured if the organization strictly reproduces the decisions taken at just one specific moment in the past.

[7] In the context of an incomplete market, Drèze (1974), followed by Grossman & Hart (1979), proposed inter-shareholder transfers inspired by Lindahl (1958) as a way to restore the only part of the welfare theorem that could be restored: Proposition 3.3. More recently, Britz et al. (2013) described a model of negotiations that underpins Drèze's criterion.

[8] See Burns (1961) or March (1962).

[9] Gevers (1974), Benninga & Muller (1979), Drèze (1985), Sadanand & Williamson (1991), DeMarzo (1993), and Kelsey & Milne (1996).

1

Disagreements on the Market

1.1 The Imperfect Market

The neoclassical model of general equilibrium provides an elegant and parsimonious demonstration of the power of the market.[1] Each consumer assigns relative values to goods based on his personal situation and preferences. The market does the same, displaying relative prices between goods. Competition between agents is seamless: goods are homogeneous and each has a price which agents believe they cannot influence, and information about the goods and their prices is available to all.

1.1.1 The Dictatorship of the Perfect Market

If an individual consumer agrees with the market prices, there is no margin for a beneficial transaction, and so no transaction takes place. If however he disagrees, then he can place those goods he deems overpriced on the market and in exchange seek those he deems underpriced. Over the course of these exchanges, because the consumer has less and less of the goods he sells, the law of diminishing marginal utility tells us that these goods become increasingly scarce in his bundle and therefore more valuable in his eyes relative to other goods; conversely the goods he buys tend to lose perceived relative value. And so the consumer gradually finds that the relative values he assigns to goods get closer and closer to the relative market prices. This continues until such time as the relative individual values and market prices coincide.[2] Trading therefore ends when everyone agrees on the relative values of the goods.

Hence disagreements between shareholders are 'cleared' on the market through trading, as is the disparity between supply and demand—the work of

---

[1] The neoclassical model of general equilibrium, first developed in the fertile mind of Walras (1874), was properly established by Arrow & Debreu (1954) and McKenzie (1954), and analysis thereof reached its apogee thirty years later; see Balasko (1988) and Mas-Colell (1985).
[2] In other words, at the optimum, the marginal rates of substitution equal out for all consumers and coincide with price ratios—see Equation 1.1.

Democracy, the Market, and the Firm: How the Interplay between Trading and Voting Fosters Political Stability and Economic Efficiency. Hervé Crès and Mich Tvede, Oxford University Press. © Hervé Crès and Mich Tvede 2021.
DOI: 10.1093/oso/9780192894731.003.0002

the so-called invisible hand. This double clearing process creates an economic equilibrium. Quite light assumptions are needed to demonstrate its existence. And luckily enough this equilibrium is *efficient* as there is no alternative which can improve the welfare of some without impairing that of others. So when everyone sets about improving their own welfare on the market, the collective result is remarkable to the extent that no central planner would be able to achieve a better outcome for all. This is the first welfare theorem.

In terms of political economy, the impact of this alignment of agents through the clearing of disagreement is immense: in particular, it rids the question of economic efficiency of any political content. If the objective is to be efficient, then enough said; if it is to be just or fair, that's a whole other story, one that is every bit as fascinating but lies outside the scope of this essay—beyond the obvious statement that markets do little for fairness.

The framework of the perfect market is useful as a benchmark model, the essence of which is presented in Section 1.2. This model is perfectly conducive to changes that account for the market's most conspicuous imperfections, such as those that appear when time and uncertainty, or the production of major firms, are introduced to the model.

1.1.2 Market Failures and Non-alignment

The model easily extends to a more refined description of goods that includes physical characteristics, location, state and date. For example, in the case of uncertainty, with the introduction of contingent goods (as in Debreu, 1959) or securities (as in Arrow, 1953), it is easy to demonstrate equivalence with the framework of the perfect market. There is a caveat, however: this requires the financial structure of the market to be complete, i.e. it must allow each individual to protect herself against all conceivable contingencies. If there are probable future states of the world to which no wealth can be transferred or between which no transaction is possible, then the financial structure of the market is incomplete, and so too is the alignment of values when trading comes to an end. Such alignment only occurs in the sub-space in which financial transfers are possible. Conversely, values are non-aligned in the (complementary) sub-space in which such transfers are impossible. The result is that agents do not agree on how to calculate profit, which leads to conflict between shareholders that must be settled one way or another. This scenario is presented in Section 1.3.

The unanimity of opinions about the value of goods also resists the introduction of production to the model. Firms belong to shareholders in the form of collective ownership, and their profits are distributed in the form of dividends. Given that shareholders (who are also consumers) agree on the value of goods, they agree on how profit is to be calculated. And if a firm's profit levels in no way affect those of another, then their shared interest is clearly to maximize those profits. But what if this is not the case? Suppose, for example, the competition is imperfect because one firm is so powerful that its production choices affect the prices of many goods on the market. All its shareholders would not necessarily want to maximize its profits.

The decision to increase profits is welcome provided it generates no externalities. If firms inflict direct production externalities on one another, whether negative—as in the case of pollution—or positive, it is a different story. Then disagreements emerge. Suppose the production of firm A affects the production (and therefore profit) of firm B; so, for example, a shareholder with equal shares in both firms will oppose a decision to increase the profits of firm A if it would result in a more substantial fall in those of firm B. It is clear that, whatever the circumstances, two shareholders with different portfolios are unlikely to agree on the best decision to make. This scenario is presented in Section 1.4.

The same phenomenon occurs when there are pecuniary externalities that would affect the value of other assets via the movement in prices. It is conceivable that a shareholder might support a decision to reduce profits if the gain to be made elsewhere, through the increased value of other assets, more than compensates for the loss. In any case, two different shareholders are unlikely to agree on the best decision to make: they are both affected in the same way by changes in the profits of the firm concerned, but in different ways by the impact of their decision on the value of the other assets they own. Imperfect competition therefore shatters the idealistic unanimity of the perfect market. The model for this is presented in Section 1.5.

1.1.3 Value Vectors

The objective of this chapter is to propose an elementary theoretical framework with which to depict the different types of market failures in a single model. The model represents a market on which a certain number of goods (ℓ) are traded. The value of these goods varies in the eyes of the different agents, each of whom, whether an individual (consumer or shareholder) or a collective entity (firm), assigns a particular value to each good using an accounting unit that is common to all agents. Each agent is depicted by a vector whose ℓ components represent the relative values assigned by that agent to the ℓ goods traded on the market. This *value vector* is expressed in different ways if the market is perfect (Equation 1.1), if its financial structure is incomplete (Equation 1.3), if the firms concerned inflict production externalities on one another (Equation 1.4), or if competition is imperfect (Equation 1.5). The notation adopted uniformly for a value vector is ∇ (nabla).

One important point constitutes an original aspect of this essay. This value vector is the central tool on which the analysis is based. It enables the politics of agreements and disagreements to be linked to the economics of individual optimization. In terms of goods, it represents the direction in which each shareholder wishes to shift production. Unanimity between shareholders is of course represented by a situation in which all value vectors are collinear and point in the same direction. The image of alignment between all stakeholders— a typically political one—here takes on its full significance.

The model's hypotheses and characteristics ensure that each production choice is associated with a single, clearly defined value vector (Lemma 1.1). This means that firms, as collective agents, implicitly indicate a particular value vector as soon as they decide on a production plan. The value vectors enable a symmetrical representation of the individual and collective agents. Furthermore, in Chapter 2, they will facilitate the incorporation into the trading model of methods and concepts borrowed from voting theory.

Section 1.2 presents the benchmark model of a perfect market, known as the Walrasian model, and the notions of equilibrium and welfare optimum. Section 1.3 introduces time and intertemporal decisions in the economy and outlines the role of financial assets and the consequences of an incomplete financial structure. Section 1.4 introduces direct external effects of production between firms. Section 1.5 focuses on the consequences of imperfect competition between firms, driven by monopolistic production. In each case of market failure, the expression of the value vector ∇ representing individual preferences will be identified. The last section will conclude that, faced with the disagreements between shareholders, there is no way out: one will have to vote.

1.2 The Benchmark Economy

The economy is represented in a stylized manner by a traditional general equilibrium model, in line with Arrow & Debreu (1954). It only includes two types of agent: consumers and firms who exchange ℓ goods. The goods are perfectly divisible, so consumption and production take place in $\mathbb{R}^\ell$. The hypotheses made in relation to the fundamental characteristics of the agents (utility function for consumers and production set for firms) are well established and will not be the subject of any further comment, so as to concentrate as much as possible on this essay's main contribution.

1.2.1 Firms

There are J firms, indexed from 1 to J, where $\mathcal{J} = \{1, \ldots, J\}$. Each firm j faces different possible ways to transform inputs into outputs. These ways are represented by a production possibility set $\mathcal{Y}_j \subset \mathbb{R}^\ell$. The production possibility set $\mathcal{Y}_j$ is assumed to be non-empty, compact and convex, and delimited by a smooth boundary, denoted $\partial \mathcal{Y}_j$: for every j there is a smooth and strictly convex function $g_j : \mathbb{R}^\ell \to \mathbb{R}$ such that

$$\mathcal{Y}_j = \{\, y_j \in \mathbb{R}^\ell \mid g_j(y_j) \leq 0 \,\}.$$

Element $y_j \in \mathcal{Y}_j$ is referred to as a production plan. Negative coordinates represent inputs and positive coordinates represent outputs. Let $y = (y_1, \ldots, y_J) \in \mathcal{Y} = \prod_j \mathcal{Y}_j$ be a list of production plans.

A simple illustration of such a production set will be employed in Chapter 3, in the case of two goods, $\ell = 2$, where $\mathcal{Y} \subset \mathbb{R}^2$ is defined by $g(y^1, y^2) = \|(y^1, y^2)\| - 1$, and $\|(\alpha, \beta)\| = \sqrt{\alpha^2 + \beta^2}$ is the Euclidean norm on $\mathbb{R}^2$; then

$$\partial \mathcal{Y} = \{y = (y^1, y^2) \in \mathbb{R}^2 \mid \|(y^1, y^2)\| = 1\}.$$

The set $\mathcal{Y}$ is therefore the disk of radius 1 centered at O, and its frontier $\partial \mathcal{Y}$ the circle of radius 1; they are represented in Fig. 1.1.

1.2.2 Consumers

There are I consumers, indexed from 1 to I, where $\mathcal{I} = \{1, \ldots, I\}$. Consumer i has preferences, which are represented by a utility function $U_i : \mathbb{R}^\ell \to \mathbb{R}$ over the space of consumption bundles; U_i is assumed to be smooth, monotonic and strictly quasi-concave. Let us denote $x_i \in \mathbb{R}^\ell$ a consumption bundle, and $x = (x_1, \ldots, x_I) \in \mathbb{R}^{\ell I}$ a list of consumption bundles.

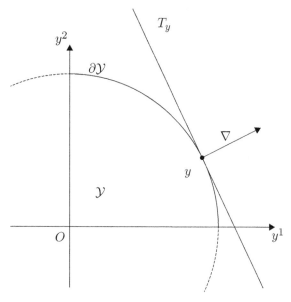

Fig. 1.1 Production

The consumer also has a vector of initial resources $\bar{x}_i = (\bar{x}_i^1, \ldots, \bar{x}_i^\ell) \in \mathbb{R}^\ell$, also referred to as an endowment, and an initial portfolio of firm shares $\bar{\theta}_i = (\bar{\theta}_{i1}, \ldots, \bar{\theta}_{iJ}) \in \mathbb{R}^J$, where $\bar{\theta}_{ij}$ represents the share held by consumer i in firm j. Exactly 100 percent of the shares are initially distributed, hence $\sum_i \bar{\theta}_{ij} = 1$ for every j. The economy is therefore described using the following data:

$$((U_i, \bar{x}_i, \bar{\theta}_i)_{i \in I}, (g_j)_{j \in J}).$$

1.2.3 Allocations and Efficiency

Let $x = (x_1, \ldots, x_I)$, where $x_i \in \mathbb{R}^\ell$ for every i, a list of bundles, and $\theta = (\theta_1, \ldots, \theta_I)$, where $\theta_i \in \mathbb{R}^J$ for every i, a list of portfolios.

Definition 1.1 *An **allocation** (x, y) is a list of bundles and plans such that $y \in \mathcal{Y}$ and aggregate supply and demand balance each other out:*

$$\sum_i x_i = \sum_i \bar{x}_i + \sum_j y_j.$$

The economic efficiency of an allocation is defined in the traditional manner using the notion of Pareto optimality.

Definition 1.2 *An allocation* (x, y) *is* **optimal** *if there is no other allocation* (x', y') *such that* $U_i(x'_i) \geq U_i(x_i)$ *for every* i, *with strict inequality for at least one* i.

1.2.4 Value Vectors

Agents (both consumers and firms) use value vectors $\nabla \in \mathbb{R}^\ell \backslash \{0\}$ to make their decisions. These vectors are in some cases normalized so that the sum of their coordinates equals 1. Let $\mathbb{S}^\ell$ be the unit simplex in $\mathbb{R}^\ell$:

$$\mathbb{S}^\ell = \left\{ \nabla \in \mathbb{R}^\ell_+ \mid \sum_s \nabla^s = 1 \right\}$$

where $\mathbb{S}^\ell_+$ denotes its interior. The normalization in $\mathbb{S}^\ell$ of the value vector ∇ is denoted as $\nabla^{\|}$.

A production plan is optimal for a firm provided it maximizes the value of production for a certain value vector.

Definition 1.3 *Plan* $y_j \in \mathcal{Y}_j$ *is a* **solution** *for value vector* ∇_j *if*

$$\nabla_j \cdot y_j \geq \nabla_j \cdot y'_j \text{ for all } y'_j \in \mathcal{Y}_j.$$

Here, it is said that ∇_j **supports** y_j.

Fig. 1.1 represents, for a plan $y \in \partial \mathcal{Y}$, the value vector ∇ which supports it: it is orthogonal to the tangent at y of $\partial \mathcal{Y}$, denoted T_y.

The following result is important. It demonstrates that in respect of our hypotheses there is a bijective relationship between value vectors and optimal plans. (Proofs are available in Appendix B.).

Lemma 1.1 *Assuming* $\mathcal{Y}_j$ *is not a singleton, then*

- $y_j \in \partial \mathcal{Y}_j$ *if and only if* $g_j(y_j) = 0$;
- $y_j \in \mathcal{Y}_j$ *is a solution for* $\nabla_j \in \mathbb{R}^\ell \setminus \{0\}$ *if and only if* $y_j \in \partial \mathcal{Y}_j$ *and* $Dg_j(y_j)$ *and* ∇_j *are collinear, and point in the same direction;*
- *for all* $y_j \in \partial \mathcal{Y}_j$ *there is a unique (up to collinearity) value vector in* $\mathbb{R}^\ell \backslash \{0\}$ *supporting* y_j; *it is denoted as* $\nabla_j(y_j)$;
- *for all* $\nabla_j \in \mathbb{R}^\ell_+ \setminus \{0\}$ *there is a unique production plan* $y_j \in \partial \mathcal{Y}_j$ *which is a solution for* ∇_j.

1.2.5 Economic Equilibrium

Let $Y = (y_1 \ldots y_J)$ denote the $\ell \times J$ matrix of production plans. The initial resources of consumer i are the addition of her endowments and the product of her initial portfolio: $\bar{x}_i + Y\bar{\theta}_i$. For a market price vector $p \in \mathbb{S}^\ell_+$, let us define the budget set of consumer i as follows:

$$B_i(p, y) = \left\{ x_i \in \mathbb{R}^\ell \mid p \cdot x_i \leq p \cdot (\bar{x}_i + Y\bar{\theta}_i) \right\}.$$

The notion of (Walrasian) equilibrium stems naturally from this.

Definition 1.4 *For plans $\bar{y} \in \mathcal{Y}$, an **equilibrium** is a vector $(p^*, x^*, \bar{y})$ where $(x^*, \bar{y})$ is an allocation, and x^* is a solution to the consumer problem: for every i,*

$$x_i^* = \arg\max\{ U_i(x_i) \mid x_i \in B_i(p^*, \bar{y})\}.$$

Of course, the general equilibrium analysis will only be complete when the choice of production plans has been determined endogenously. This will be achieved in the next chapter, where firm decisions will reflect the will of consumers, whether shareholders or stakeholders.

One crucial point is to determine whether shareholders or stakeholders agree on what firms should produce. They agree if and only if all normalized value vectors used to take decisions are identical.

1.2.6 When Consumers Are Unanimous

The form of the budget set $B_i(p, y)$ implies that consumer i evaluates firm j's plans based on the value of the shares he holds: $\bar{\theta}_{ij}p \cdot y_j$. The greater this value, the better. Furthermore, at equilibrium the first-order conditions of the optimization problem for consumers are such that the values of goods as perceived by them (marginal utility, represented by the gradient $DU_i(x_i)$ for shareholder i) and the values of goods as priced by the market equalize (the proof of this elementary result is omitted). This means all consumers agree to use the market prices to evaluate production plans, and for every i, the normalized value vector (or gradient) equals the price vector:

$$\boxed{\nabla_i^\| = p^*} \tag{1.1}$$

They are fully aligned and therefore all agree on the best plan, i.e. that which maximizes the value of production based on market prices. The notion of general equilibrium follows on from this.

Definition 1.5 *A **general equilibrium** (p^*, x^*, y^*) is an equilibrium at which production plans of firms maximize profits for the equilibrium prices: for every j*

$$y_j^* = \arg\max \{p^* \cdot y_j \mid y_i \in \mathcal{Y}_j\}.$$

And it gets better. Not only do consumers agree on the best production plan, but such a plan also supports an optimal allocation. This is the first welfare theorem: for a general equilibrium (p^*, x^*, y^*), then equilibrium allocation (x^*, y^*) is optimal. And the second welfare theorem is also valid: given an optimal allocation, there are initial conditions $(\bar{x}_i, \bar{\theta}_i)_{i \in \mathcal{I}}$ under which the considered allocation is an equilibrium allocation.

1.2.7 A Textbook Scenario: Quadratic Utilities

By way of illustration, let us consider the following quadratic utility function which will be extensively employed in Chapter 3:

$$U_i(x_i) = \sum_{s=1}^{\ell} \pi^s \left(\gamma_i x_i^s - \frac{1}{2}(x_i^s)^2 \right) \tag{1.2}$$

where $\pi = (\pi^1, \ldots, \pi^\ell) \in \mathbb{S}_+^\ell$ are weightings attributed to the different goods (independently of i), and $\gamma_i \in \mathbb{R}_+$ is a parameter. Let $\Omega = \sum_i \bar{x}_i + \sum_j y_j$ be the vector for the overall resources of the economy. We assume that for every i, $\gamma_i > \max\{\Omega^s, 1 \leq s \leq \ell\}$ such that the utility function satisfies the required hypotheses (e.g., monotonicity) on the set of relevant consumptions.

Let $\| \cdot \|_\pi$ denote the π-norm[3] on $\mathbb{R}^\ell$. Let $\mathbf{1}_\ell$ (respectively $\mathbf{1}_J$) be the vector with ℓ (respectively J) coordinates, all equal to 1. Therefore

$$U_i(x_i) = \frac{1}{2}\gamma_i^2 - \frac{1}{2}\|\gamma_i \mathbf{1}_\ell - x_i\|_\pi^2.$$

---

[3] Let us define the following bilinear form on $\mathbb{R}^\ell \times \mathbb{R}^\ell$: $y \times_\pi z = \sum_s \pi^s y^s z^s$. This defines a norm on $\mathbb{R}^\ell$ (if π has positive coordinates):

$$\|y - z\|_\pi = \sqrt{\sum_{s=1}^{\ell} \pi^s (y^s - z^s)^2}.$$

The indifference (hyper)surfaces of consumer i are (hyper)spheres for the π-distance, centered on $\gamma_i 1_\ell$, which hence represents the *ideal bundle* for this consumer, the one that maximizes $U_i(x_i)$ and that she would choose if there were no constraint of resources or budget.

Fig. 1.2 illustrates the configuration in the case of two goods and equal weights: $\pi^1 = \pi^2 = 0.5$ (Euclidean distance). Indifference curves are arcs of a circle centered on $\gamma_i 1_\ell$. At the individual optimum x_i^*, the indifference curve is tangential to the budget line, determined by the vector of initial resources $\bar{x}_i + Y\bar{\theta}_i$ and orthogonal to the price vector p, which bounds the budget set $B_i(p, y)$.

Let Π be the diagonal matrix whose size is ℓ with π on the diagonal, then the gradient takes the following form:

$$\nabla_i = DU_i(x_i) = \Pi(\gamma_i 1_\ell - x_i).$$

The indifference surfaces being (elliptic) hyperspheres, the gradient points towards the center of the hypersphere of indifference, i.e. the ideal bundle. (In Fig. 1.2, at the individual optimum x_i^*, the normalized gradient $\nabla_i^{\|} = p$ points toward the center of the arcs of circle $\gamma_i 1_\ell$.)

The Walrasian equilibrium price vector is easy to calculate. Define $\Gamma = \sum_i \gamma_i$.

Lemma 1.2 *At equilibrium, one has*

$$p^* = \frac{1}{\Gamma - \pi \cdot \Omega} \Pi(\Gamma 1_\ell - \Omega),$$

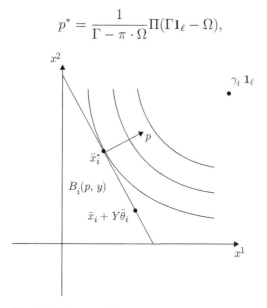

Fig. 1.2 Consumption

and there exist $(\alpha_i^*)_{i \in \mathcal{I}} \in \mathbb{S}_+^I$ *such that for every* i, $x_i^* = \gamma_i 1_\ell - \alpha_i^* (\Gamma 1_\ell - \Omega)$.

It is easy to verify that at equilibrium the gradients are all collinear:

$$\nabla_i^* = DU_i(x_i^*) = \alpha_i^* \Pi (\Gamma 1_\ell - \Omega).$$

The results lends itself to a quite simple and intuitive geometrical interpretation. The bundle $\gamma_i 1_\ell$ being the ideal bundle of consumer i, her *ideal transaction is* $\check{z}_i = \gamma_i 1_\ell - (\bar{x}_i + Y \bar{\theta}_i)$; and the aggregate ideal transaction is $\check{z} = \sum_i \check{z}_i = \Gamma 1_\ell - \Omega$.

The equilibrium bundle $x_i^* = \gamma_i 1_\ell - \alpha_i^* \check{z}$ is therefore the ideal bundle decreased by a proportion of the ideal aggregate transaction. This proportion is

$$\alpha_i^* = \frac{\check{z} \times_\pi \check{z}_i}{\|\check{z}\|_\pi^2} \text{ for every } i$$

(cf. proof of Lemma 1.2). The proportion α_i^* measures the π−projection of the ideal transaction of i on the ideal aggregate transaction. The less $\check{z}_i$ is collinear to $\check{z}$ (a situation where consumer i's ideal transaction *diversifies* the aggregate ideal transaction) the smaller α_i^*, and thus the larger the equilibrium bundle. In this model a consumer is rewarded if her transaction diversifies the economy.

1.2.8 Conclusion

In conclusion of this first subsection, we can see that complete alignment between consumers stems from the hypothesis of a perfect market, thus ridding the decision-making process in firms of any political content. This is no longer the case when markets fail. Consumers then disagree about the plan to produce. In our model, this occurs when the $\nabla_i^\|$s are different from one agent to another, giving rise to a problem of a political nature when it comes to taking collective decisions, like choosing the production plans in firms.

Let us begin by studying the case of an incomplete market on which consumers generally disagree about how to calculate the value of production.

1.3 The Incomplete Market

The economy includes two dates $t \in \{0, 1\}$, whereby date 1 represents an uncertain future, with ℓ possible states of the world $s \in \{1, \ldots, \ell\}$. In order to simplify the model as much as possible, we will exclude consumption on date 0 and imagine that there is only one consumer good in each state of the world on date 1. As in the previous section, the consumption and production space is therefore represented by set $\mathbb{R}^\ell$ of real vectors with ℓ coordinates. The firms' production plans are here assets which the agents trade on financial markets.

The equation $x_i = \bar{x}_i + Y\theta_i$ (portfolio θ_i is said to finance bundle x_i) means that (x, y) is an allocation if and only if the demand and supply of shares clear:

$$\sum_i \theta_i = \sum_i \bar{\theta}_i = 1_J.$$

One can easily check that

$$\sum_i \theta_i = 1_J \Longrightarrow \sum_i x_i = \sum_i \bar{x}_i + \sum_j y_j.$$

1.3.1 Value Vectors

A marginal change Δy_j of production in firm j changes the utility of consumer i:

$$U_i(x_i + \theta_{ij}\Delta y_j) - U_i(x_i) \simeq \theta_{ij} DU_i(x_i) \cdot \Delta y_j.$$

As a result, the value vector of consumer i in firm j takes the following form:

$$\boxed{\nabla_{ij}(x_i) = \theta_{ij} DU_i(x_i)} \tag{1.3}$$

Therefore, if $\theta_{ij} > 0$, the normalized value vector of consumer i is

$$\nabla_i^\| = \frac{1}{DU_i(x_i) \cdot 1_\ell} DU_i(x_i).$$

This is the present value vector of consumer i. It is the vector which, as a shareholder in firm j, consumer i uses to evaluate and choose the production plan, as established by the following result.

Lemma 1.3 *For consumer i and firm j, where $\theta_{ij} > 0$, given a marginal change in production $\Delta y_j \in \mathbb{R}^\ell$:*

- *If $U_i(x_i + \theta_{ij}\Delta y_j) > U_i(x_i)$, then $\nabla_i^\|(x_i) \cdot \Delta y_j > 0$.*
- *If $\nabla_i^\|(x_i) \cdot \Delta y_j > 0$, then there is $t_i > 0$ such that $U_i(x_i + t\theta_{ij}\Delta y_j) > U_i(x_i)$ for all $t \in]0, t_i[$.*

The second assertion in Lemma 1.3 is the *principle of minimal differentiation*: when a proposal is made to change production in a firm, it can only gain the support of more shareholders when the deviation from the status quo is scaled down (when the deviation $t\Delta y$ is proposed, the smaller t the more shareholders i for whom $t < t_i$). The most compelling alternatives to the status quo are infinitesimal deviations from it. The principle of minimal differentiation has an important consequence: the analysis based on the value vectors ∇ instead of utility functions *still has a global reach*.

Contrary to the case of a perfect market, if the financial market is incomplete, no condition of general equilibrium can guarantee alignment between shareholders. We will now turn our attention to this.

1.3.2 Equilibrium

In this simple financial model, consumers trade assets on date 0. The prices of the J assets are represented by vector $q = (q_1, \ldots, q_J)$, where q_j is the price of asset j.

Given prices q and plans y, consumers trade on the market so as to maximize their level of utility. The budget set of consumer i is

$$\tilde{B}_i(q, y) = \left\{ x_i \in \mathbb{R}^\ell \mid \exists \theta_i \in \mathbb{R}^J \text{ such that } q \cdot \theta_i \leq q \cdot \bar{\theta}_i \text{ and } x_i = \bar{x}_i + Y\theta_i \right\}.$$

A simple notion of (financial) equilibrium stems naturally from Definition 1.4.

Definition 1.6 *For plans $\bar{y}$, an equilibrium is a vector $(q^*, x^*, \bar{y})$ where $(x^*, \bar{y})$ is an allocation, and x^* is a solution to the consumer problem: for every i,*

$$x_i^* = \arg\max\{ U_i(x_i) \mid x_i \in \tilde{B}_i(q^*, \bar{y})\}.$$

It should be noted that the hypothesis that agents behave competitively excludes all strategic considerations in choosing their portfolios.

The geometry of the equilibrium gradients and net trades is simple and transparent. Let $\langle Y \rangle$ be the vectorial space spanned by Y; the first-order conditions of consumer i's optimization problem yield the following result.

Lemma 1.4 *At equilibrium $(q^*, x^*, \bar{y})$, for every i*

$$x_i^* - \bar{x}_i \in \langle Y \rangle \text{ and } Y^T DU_i(x_i^*) \text{ is collinear to } q^*.$$

Lemma 1.4 states that at equilibrium the net trade $x_i^* - \bar{x}_i$ must be financially engineered, i.e. has to be in the asset span; and all consumers agree with each other, and agree with the market, on how to evaluate portfolios: $Y^T DU_i^{\|} = q^{*\|}$ (the superscript $^{\|}$ standing for normalization). As a consequence, all consumers agree on how to evaluate transfers in the asset span $\langle Y \rangle$: they all use the market price on the underlying portfolio.

The market is complete when Y has rank ℓ (and by necessity $J \geq \ell$); this corresponds to a situation in which all resource transfers between the different states of the world on date 1 are possible. The market is incomplete when Y has at most rank $\ell-1$; here, certain resource transfers between the different states of the world on date 1 are impossible.

When the market is complete, the consumers' normalized value vectors are all identical. In the reverse scenario, this is no longer necessarily the case. Let us consider each scenario in turn.

1.3.3 Complete Market: Alignment between Consumers

When the market is complete, Lemma 1.4 means that the equilibrium value vectors are all identical: for every i

$$\nabla_i^{\|}(x_i^*) = \nabla^*,$$

where ∇^* is the only vector in $\mathbb{S}_+^\ell$ such that $Y^T \nabla^* = q^*$ (which implicitly normalizes q^*).

Then the budget sets for the financial economy and for the Walrasian economy coincide, which induces an equivalence between the benchmark model and the financial economy.

Lemma 1.5 *Assuming the market is complete, and considering the equilibrium* $(q^*, x^*, \bar{y})$, *let* ∇^* *denote the only vector in* $\mathbb{S}_+^\ell$ *such that* $Y^T \nabla^* = q^*$. *Then:*

$$\tilde{B}_i(q^*, y) \equiv B_i(\nabla^*, y).$$

Here, consumers all agree on how to evaluate firm returns. What is more, they all agree that these returns should be maximized, as shown in Lemma 1.5: a higher present value $\nabla \cdot y_j$ means a broader budget set from which to choose, and therefore higher utility at the optimum.

This complete alignment between consumers enables production plans to be determined endogenously in the spirit of Definition 1.5.

Definition 1.7 *A general (financial) equilibrium* (q^*, x^*, y^*) *is an equilibrium such that for every j*

$$y_j^* = \arg\max \left\{ \nabla^* \cdot y_j \mid y_j \in \mathcal{Y}_j \right\}.$$

What happens if the market is incomplete?

1.3.4 Incomplete Market: Only Partial Alignment between Consumers

To simplify matters, let us assume that the firm's shares are not traded: $\theta_i = \bar{\theta}_i$. The consumers are then self-isolated and only consume their initial resources: $x_i = \bar{x}_i + Y\bar{\theta}_i$. The value vectors are the normalized gradients $(\nabla_i^{\parallel}(\bar{x}_i + Y\bar{\theta}_i))_{i \in \mathcal{I}}$. It is easy to demonstrate that generically, i.e. for almost all the initial conditions $(\bar{x}_i, \bar{\theta}_i)_{i \in \mathcal{I}}$, the vectors $(\nabla_i^{\parallel}(\bar{x}_i + Y\bar{\theta}_i))_{i \in \mathcal{I}}$ are in general position, meaning they create a linear space of full dimension $\min\{\ell - 1, I\}$. Here, consumers disagree about how to evaluate any asset (except null assets). The extent of the conflict between them is therefore at its maximum.

When shares are traded, Lemma 1.4 does not guarantee that at equilibrium consumers will agree on the evaluation of all transfers (in other words, their normalized gradients are not all equal) but the extent of the conflict between them is not as extreme as in the self-isolation scenario. Trading requires partial alignment between consumers as they all agree on how to evaluate transfers in the asset span $\langle Y \rangle$. The disagreements between them persist, for sure, but they are residual insofar as they only manifest themselves when it comes to evaluating transfers outside of the asset span.

The extent of the conflict between shareholders is nonetheless significant, given that the conditions of Lemma 1.4 are still such that the value vectors can be different in twos, as in the self-isolation scenario. This is clear from the following proposition.

Proposition 1.1 *Assume there are at least two consumers ($I \geq 2$) and that the market is incomplete. Fix $\bar{y}$, then for every equilibrium $(q^*, x^*, \bar{y})$ and for almost all the endowments $\bar{x}$, the consumers' present value vectors are different pairwise:*

$$\nabla_i^{\parallel}(x_i^*) \neq \nabla_{i'}^{\parallel}(x_{i'}^*) \ if \ i \neq i'.$$

Ultimately, the market only partially fulfills its mission to align shareholders: it only eliminates conflicts between them in the sub-space of financial transfers. If this space takes on its full dimension (complete market), then the conflicts are fully eliminated; otherwise they are just partially eliminated, in which case it is conceptually problematic for production plans to be determined endogenously, as a collective decision-making mechanism must be used to settle disagreements.

This discussion illustrates how it is possible to assert that the market helps reduce conflicts between shareholders: it reduces the number of conflict *dimensions*. The consequences of this will be explored in Section 3.4.

1.3.5 Return to the Textbook Scenario

Let us go back to the quadratic utility functions (1.2), interpreted here as *expected* utility functions, where π is an objective probability distribution over states of the world on date 1, common to all agents. The preferences are therefore mean-variance preferences with a linear tolerance for risk, as in the Capital Asset Pricing Model (CAPM).

Lemma 1.6 *Let* (q^*, x^*, θ^*) *be a general equilibrium. Let* $P_{\langle Y \rangle}$ *denote the* π-*projection onto the space of market transfers.*[4] *There exist* $(\alpha_i^*)_{i \in \mathcal{I}} \in \mathbb{S}_+^I$ *such that for every* i,

$$x_i^* = \bar{x}_i + (\gamma_i - \alpha_i^* \Gamma) P_{\langle Y \rangle} 1_\ell - P_{\langle Y \rangle} (\bar{x}_i - \alpha_i^* \Omega).$$

In the case of a complete market, the matrix $P_{\langle Y \rangle}$ is the identity mapping, which brings us back to the Walrasian bundle in Lemma 1.2: for every i,

$$x_i^{*w} = (\gamma_i - \alpha_i^* \Gamma) 1_\ell + \alpha_i^* \Omega,$$

which confirms the linear-sharing rule, i.e. that at equilibrium each consumer only invests in the risk-free asset 1_ℓ and the market portfolio Ω.

Let us assume that $\bar{x}_i \in \langle Y \rangle$ for every i and $1_\ell \in \langle Y \rangle$. In this case, the incompleteness of the markets has no consequence as the available assets

---

[4] The π-projection of vector z onto $\langle Y \rangle$ is defined as the vector of $\langle Y \rangle$ that is closest to z for the π-distance. Its matrical expression is $P_{\langle Y \rangle} = Y \left(Y^T \Pi Y \right)^{-1} Y^T \Pi$ (see Magill & Quinzii, 1996).

provide protection against the exogenous shocks represented by the endowments. The equilibrium bundle is therefore the Walrasian bundle: $x_i^* = x_i^{*w}$.

On the contrary, if there is an i such that $\bar{x}_i \notin \langle Y \rangle$, then the equilibrium bundle is no longer the Walrasian bundle. Yet the geometry of the problem remains transparent and intuitive; the optimal bundle is obtained for the net trade (in the space $\langle Y \rangle$):

$$x_i^* - \bar{x}_i = P_{\langle Y \rangle} \left(x_i^{*w} - \bar{x}_i \right),$$

which, for the π-distance, is the closest to the Walrasian net trade $x_i^{*w} - \bar{x}_i$. Therefore, the market does as well as possible given its incompleteness.

1.4 Production Externalities

The modelling of production needs to be slightly amended in order to circumvent certain technical difficulties (Crès & Tvede, 2013). Firms are represented not by their production sets but by sets of possible decisions $A_j \subset \mathbb{R}^d$ and functions of production $f_j : A \to \mathbb{R}^\ell$, where $A = \prod_j A_j$. Plan $y_j = f_j(a)$ for firm j stems from a list of decisions $a = (a_1, \ldots, a_J)$, such that the production of each firm depends on the decisions taken in *all* firms, and the production matrix will be denoted $Y(a)$. We assume that A_j is defined by a function $g_j : \mathbb{R}^d \to \mathbb{R}$ such that $A_j = \{a_j \in \mathbb{R}^d \mid g_j(a_j) \leq 0\}$. This gives us an economy described using the data

$$\left((U_i, \bar{x}_i, \bar{\theta}_i)_{i \in \mathcal{I}}, (f_j, g_j)_{j \in \mathcal{J}} \right).$$

When firms inflict externalities on one another and there is no market with which to internalize them, in general shareholders do not necessarily seek to maximize profits. Supposing firm j pollutes firm j', shareholders with stock only in firm j will be indifferent to the pollution and most likely seek to maximize the profits of firm j, but the shareholders of firm j' will not necessarily follow the same path.

So even though the markets enable all consumers to equalize the marginal rates of substitution between the different goods, resulting in their alignment on how to calculate profits, not all shareholders will generally agree that those profits should be maximized.

1.4.1 The Interdependence of Profits

Based on the hypothesis of competitive behavior among agents, a change in the decisions taken by firm j only affects consumers in terms of dividends $p \cdot f_j(a)$. This means that consumer i prefers decision a'_j over decision a_j in firm j if and only if his dividends increase:

$$p \cdot Y(a'_j, a_{-j})\bar{\theta}_i > p \cdot Y(a)\bar{\theta}_i$$

where $a = (a_j, a_{-j})$ and $a_{-j} = (a_1, \cdots, a_{j-1}, a_{j+1}, \cdots, a_J)$.

An infinitesimal change $da_j = (da_j^k)_{k=1}^d$ in the decisions of firm j changes the plan in firm j' from $y_{j'}$ to $y_{j'} + D_{a_j} f_{j'}(a) da_j$, where $D_{a_j} f_{j'}(a)$ is the $\ell \times d$ Jacobian matrix for $f_{j'}$ with respect to a_j. Hence it affects the profits $p \cdot f_{j'}(a)$ of firm j' according to the matrical expression

$$\sum_{k=1}^d \left(p \cdot \frac{\partial f_{j'}(a)}{\partial a_j^k} \right) da_j^k = (D_{a_j} f_{j'}(a)^T p) \cdot da_j.$$

Here, the vector $D_{a_j} f_{j'}(a)^T p \in \mathbb{R}^d$ measures the extent to which a (marginal) change in the decisions of firm j affects the profits of firm j'.

Depending on their portfolios $\bar{\theta}_i$, consumers will weigh up the costs and benefits of a change of decisions in different ways. Once again, all of the useful information is contained in the value vector.

1.4.2 Value Vectors

A marginal change in decisions Δa_j hence results in a change in the revenue of consumer i, expressed as

$$\sum_{j'} \bar{\theta}_{ij'} D_{a_j} f_{j'}(a)^T p \cdot \Delta a_j = \nabla_{ij}(p, a) \cdot \Delta a_j.$$

The value vector of consumer i therefore takes the following form:[5]

$$\nabla_{ij}(p, a) = \sum_{j'} \bar{\theta}_{ij'} D_{a_j} f_{j'}(a)^T p.$$

---

[5] The Walrasian scenario in Section 1.2 can easily be recovered. If we assume there are no production externalities, i.e. $d = \ell$ and for every j, $\mathcal{A}_j \equiv \mathcal{Y}_j$ and $f_j(a) = a_j = y_j$, then $D_{a_j} f_{j'}(a) = 0$ for $j' \neq j$ and $D_{a_j} f_j(a) = Id$, such that $\nabla_{ij}(p, a) = \bar{\theta}_{ij} p$, which means all consumers have identical (normalized) value vectors.

Let us define the $d \times J$ matrix

$$\Xi_j(p, a) = \left(D_{a_j} f_1(a)^T p \ \cdots \ D_{a_j} f_J(a)^T p \right).$$

For every i and j, this gives us:

$$\boxed{\nabla_{ij}(p, a) = \Xi_j \bar{\theta}_i} \tag{1.4}$$

The following lemma shows the equivalence between the fact that consumer i prefers decision a'_j over decision a_j in firm j and the fact that she evaluates a'_j more highly via ∇_{ij}.

Lemma 1.7 *Consider* (p, a). *For* $a'_j \neq a_j$ *and for consumer* i, *one obtains*

$$p \cdot Y(a'_j, a_{-j})\bar{\theta}_i > p \cdot Y(a)\bar{\theta}_i \implies \nabla_{ij}(p, a) \cdot a'_j > \nabla_{ij}(p, a) \cdot a_j.$$

Reciprocally, there is $t_{ij} \in]0, 1]$ *such that* $\forall\, t \in]0, t_{ij}[$,

$$\nabla_{ij}(p, a) \cdot a'_j > \nabla_{ij}(p, a) \cdot a_j \implies p \cdot Y(a_j(t), a_{-j})\bar{\theta}_i > p \cdot Y(a)\bar{\theta}_i,$$

where $a_j(t) = (1 - t)a_j + ta'_j$.

As in the case of an incomplete market, the principle of minimal differentiation follows as an immediate consequence of the second assertion in Lemma 1.7, resulting in the following property: given price vector p, portfolio $\bar{\theta}$, and decision a_{-j}, maximizing dividend $p \cdot Y(a'_j, a_{-j})\bar{\theta}$ is equivalent to maximizing the value of production with respect to $\nabla_j = \Xi_j\bar{\theta}$. The idiosyncratic element in the value vector of consumer i is her portfolio $\bar{\theta}_i$, specifically how $\bar{\theta}_i$ distributes the interdependence of profits in the different firms. The role played by portfolios will be studied in Section 3.2.

In the generic scenario,[6] consumers disagree about the best production plan; the value vectors $\nabla_{ij}^{\|}$ differ from one shareholder to another, and there is no immediate way to determine the best production plan for the firm. Once again, a collective decision-making mechanism is needed to settle the matter.

---

[6] One particular scenario is where all consumers hold the market portfolio: $\bar{\theta}_i = \alpha_i \mathbf{1}_J$ for a particular $\alpha_i \in \mathbb{R}_+$. In this case, $\nabla_{ij}(p, a) = \alpha_i \Xi_j \mathbf{1}_J$ and so all consumers have identical (normalized) value vectors.

1.5 Imperfect Competition

If a firm has market power, i.e. where its size or the volume of its transactions enable it to influence prices, then a change in production affects the wealth of consumers through two channels: profit levels; and price movements and the way in which these movements affect the value of transactions. Whereas the first channel affects the wealth of all consumers in the same way, different consumers will be affected by the second channel in different ways. This leads to the potential for disagreement between shareholders, or between stakeholders, over what constitute the best production choices.

To keep the argument as simple as possible, let us consider a version of the benchmark model with only one firm, which behaves monopolistically.[7]

1.5.1 The Demand Function

Let h_i be the demand function for consumer i, stemming from the optimization problem. This is a diffeomorphism (see Balasko, 1988) of $\mathbb{S} \times \mathbb{R}$ in $\mathbb{R}^\ell$:

$$h_i(p, w_i) = \arg\max\left\{u_i(x_i) \mid p \cdot x_i \leq w_i\right\}.$$

Given that the monopolist influences prices, consumers expect changes in its production plan to affect prices. So when they anticipate a change Δy, they will measure not only the effect of this change on the profit level but also the effect of the resulting price change on the value of transactions. To simplify, we will limit the analysis to situations in which the link between the change in the plan and the price change is defined in a unique and differentiable manner. This is the case at so-called *regular* equilibria.

1.5.2 Regular Equilibria and Price Selection

Each plan y determines a pure exchange economy in which the initial resources of consumer i are $\bar{x}_i + \bar{\theta}_i y$. Let $\check{p} : \mathcal{Y} \to \mathbb{S}^\ell$ be the equilibrium correspondence of this economy: $p \in \check{p}(y)$ if and only if (p, x, y) is an equilibrium, where $x_i = h_i(p, p \cdot (\bar{x}_i + \bar{\theta}_i y))$ for every i.

Let us consider the net aggregate demand

$$H_y(p) = -y + \sum_{i \in \mathcal{I}} h_i(p, p \cdot (\bar{x}_i + \bar{\theta}_i y)) - \bar{x}_i.$$

For a plan y, $p \in \check{p}(y)$ if and only if $H_y(p) = 0$.

---

[7] A version of the considered problem with a few oligopolists is presented in Crès & Tvede (2020).

According to Walras's law, $p \cdot H_y(p) = 0$. Therefore, if we know the $\ell - 1$ first coordinates of H_y, then we know the ℓth. Let $\mathring{H}_y$ denote the $\ell - 1$ first coordinates of H_y. For plan y, let us define the following application:

$$\mathring{H}_y : \quad \mathbb{S} \quad \to \quad \mathbb{R}^{\ell-1}$$
$$p \quad \to \quad \mathring{H}_y(p)$$

We will be focusing on regular equilibria, i.e. those at which the implicit function theorem applies to $\mathring{H}_y$.

Definition 1.8 *An equilibrium (p^*, x^*, y) is **regular** if and only if the rank of $D\mathring{H}_y(p^*)$ is $\ell - 1$.*

A limitation of this approach is that the analysis of the consequences of a change in production can only be carried out locally. That said, in the vicinity of a regular equilibrium price vector $p^* \in \breve{p}(y)$, a marginal change in production Δy results in a marginal price change Δp, according to the simple expression: $\Delta p = D_y \breve{p}^T \Delta y$, where $D_y \breve{p}$ is the $\ell \times \ell$ Jacobian matrix of $\breve{p}$ with respect to y. Denote it Φ. This makes it easy to calculate the price and income effects in determining the value vectors.

1.5.3 Value Vectors

Let $z_i = \bar{x}_i + \bar{\theta}_i y - x_i$ be the net trade of consumer i.

Proposition 1.2 *At a regular equilibrium consumer i favors a change Δy if and only if*

$$(\bar{\theta}_i p^* - \Phi z_i^*) \cdot \Delta y > 0.$$

The value vector for consumer i is therefore

$$\boxed{\nabla_i(p^*, x_i^*, y) = \bar{\theta}_i p^* - \Phi z_i^*} \tag{1.5}$$

Consumer i's support for change Δy will depend on the combination of the income effect $\bar{\theta}_i p^* \cdot \Delta y$ and the price effect $-\Phi z_i^* \cdot \Delta y$.[8] The idiosyncratic

---

[8] The Walrasian scenario can be recovered by asserting that (the agents believe that) the firm has no influence on prices: $\Phi = 0$. In this case, $\nabla_i(p, y) = \bar{\theta}_i p^*$ and all consumers have identical (normalized) value vectors.

elements in the value vector for consumer i are the net trade z_i^* and the size of the income effect. The role played by this net trade will be studied in Section 3.3.

In the generic scenario,[9] consumers disagree about the best production plan. The value vectors $\nabla_i^\|$ differ from one consumer to another, and there is no immediate way to determine the best production plan for the firm. Here, too, a collective decision-making mechanism is needed to settle the matter.

1.6 Let Us Vote Then

The market works wonders, and the alignment of values through trade is one of them. It is true that here we are only talking about commercial rather than ethical or moral values, but the alignment of values through trade is nonetheless an ideal that it is important to remember when considering the political world, which covers all values. Up to what point does this alignment through trade occur? Perhaps it extends further than we think, as the two meanings of the word *commerce* appear to suggest: buying and selling, of course, but also 'dealings, social intercourse'...and even another type of intercourse (see *OED*)!

But, like all human institutions, the market has its limits and failures. The invisible hand is not invincible. And many market failures are brought about by externalities, whether due to the presence of public goods, non-competitive behavior, financial incompleteness or information asymmetries. These externalities can be direct or indirect, technological, reputational or pecuniary, driven by prices or by the financial structure, but in any case they undermine the efficiency of the market and impede the optimal allocation of resources. The ideal scenario would be to reduce them.

1.6.1 The Invisible Hand Cannot Do It Alone

The first reflex of economists is not to adapt to these failures or to circumvent them, but instead to repair them. But how? By creating other markets, or substitute markets, and then adopting a laissez-faire approach. Sometimes they

---

[9] One particular scenario is where the initial conditions $(\bar{x}_i, \bar{\theta}_i)_{i \in I}$ are such that the allocation $((\bar{x}_i + \bar{\theta}_i y)_{i \in I}, y)$ is Pareto-optimal, in which case there is a single equilibrium (see Balasko, 1988), a *no-trade equilibrium*: $x_i^* = \bar{x}_i + \bar{\theta}_i y$ for every i. Then, $\nabla_i(p, y) = \bar{\theta}_i p^*$: consumers/shareholders are all aligned.

are more or less successful, as in the case of carbon and sulfur dioxide emission permits.[10] Perhaps this is immoral in light of the principle that some goods should remain outside the scope of the market,[11] but at any rate it goes some way towards relying on the invisible hand.

The invisible hand, as if by custom, operates through a price system. The trouble is that this system depends on prices varying based on individual determinants that cannot be observed, known as personalized prices. So the markets are threatened by a moral hazard that defeats the very purpose of their creation. What we struggle to restore on one side is ruined on the other. And to top it off, through self-fulfilling prophecies, these markets are capable of generating unequal treatment which cannot be justified on any economic basis,[12] and in turn fluctuations[13] that can worsen economic instability. In short, such decentralized mechanisms, whether they operate through trading or negotiations, are too sophisticated (and therefore costly) and/or too exposed to the risk of manipulation. They should only be used as a last resort, when no simpler alternative is satisfactory. The concept of personalized prices is nonetheless useful to reflect on, as can be seen from our value vectors.

1.6.2 A Helping Hand from Democracy Is Needed

The word failure is harsh, and morally charged. Rather than failures, we could talk of partial successes. The market often does no more than partially eliminate conflicts between shareholders, partially favor productive efficiency, or partially stabilize the strategic paths taken by firms. It needs a backup, another institution to which it can pass the baton. This is where democracy in the firm comes in, a term that refers to the majority principle in decisions made at GAs.

So let us pursue this avenue further and study democracy at work in firms. To this end, it would be useful to take a detour via social choice theory, if only to borrow a few theorems that will shed some light and allow us to move forward. This is the purpose of Chapter 2.

---

[10] Lindahl (1958), Samuelson (1954), Coase (1960) and Arrow (1969) initiated the school of thought that led to this achievement, which later inspired Drèze (1974) to propose a measurement with a view to addressing the incompleteness of the market: inter-shareholder transfers. More recently, Bisin & Gottardi (2006) suggested a similar approach to internalize information externalities on the insurance market and reduce the perverse effects of adverse selection.

[11] This does not mean that economists have nothing to say on the matter. See, for example, economic research on organ exchange (Roth et al., 2004).

[12] See Malinvaud (1972, 1973) and Crès & Rossi (2000) on individual risks, Champsaur (1978) on public goods, Crès (1996) on externalities, and Balasko (1990) for a generic approach to these breakdowns in symmetry.

[13] See Crès et al. (1997).

2
Democracy in the Firm

2.1 The Imperfect Democracy

The economic theory on individual decision-making offers a rich panorama
in which all the wealth of the living world is expressed. It offers a multitude
of theorems representing individual choices, of increasingly elaborate models
and more refined axioms—a conceptual fertility which allows us to engage
mathematical rigor in an effort to understand individual behaviors based on
rationality that comes in many guises.

The contrast between this panorama and that of the theory on collective
choice is striking.[1] One might even say that the latter is a terrain that is riddled
with paradoxes and impossibility theorems, with only the rarest positive
findings bringing a message of hope that something other than unreasoned
chaos can emerge from the aggregation of individual choices.

This contrast culminates in the contemplation of the profound and powerful
theorems of Savage (1954) on the one hand and Arrow (1951) on the other.
The former from an entanglement of axioms magically gives rise to individual
rationality in the simple and elegant form of expected utility. The latter uses
three simple axioms to extinguish all hope of collective rationality and has
become a "phantom [which] has stalked the classrooms and seminars in
economics and and political science" for nearly sixty years according to Tullock
(1967, p. 256).

Notably, and quite to the point of the present essay, Arrow's celebrated
Impossibility Theorem stemmed from his attempts to generalize the theory of
the firm with multiple owners: "To be sure, it could be assumed that all were
seeking to maximize profits; but suppose they had different expectations of the
future? They would then have different preferences over investment projects.
I first supposed that they would decide, as the legal framework would imply,

---

[1] This contrast began to take shape in the eighteenth century, through the ingenious intuitions of
Bernoulli (1738) on the one hand, and those of Condorcet (1785) on the other; it became more stark
in the twentieth century with the seminal research of de Finetti (1937), von Neumann & Morgenstern
(1944) and Savage (1954) on the one hand, and Arrow (1951) and Sen (1970) on the other.

*Democracy, the Market, and the Firm: How the Interplay between Trading and Voting Fosters Political Stability and
Economic Efficiency*. Hervé Crès and Mich Tvede, Oxford University Press. © Hervé Crès and Mich Tvede 2021.
DOI: 10.1093/oso/9780192894731.003.0003

by majority voting ... It was immediately clear that majority voting did not necessarily lead to an ordering" (Arrow, 1984, pp. 2–3).[2]

2.1.1 Failing Democracy

This pessimism can be traced back to the sophisticated mathematical work of Condorcet (1785), which is habitually explained in the simplest of manners using eponymous cycles. Imagine three partners in a firm, a, b and c, who must establish a hierarchy within their collective entity, for example the executive director and her deputy. Each partner has a specific view of the ideal hierarchy, and each one proposes to be at the top. Now assume that they have the following preferences (where $a \succ b$ means that a is preferred to b):

$$(a): a \succ b \succ c \qquad (b): b \succ c \succ a \qquad (c): c \succ a \succ b$$

The individual preferences represent a ranking of all candidates. They are assumed to be *complete*[3] and *transitive*.[4] If these voters rank the candidates two by two, then a majority of two out of three vote for a over b, b over c, and c over a; a cycle (of length three) emerges at the aggregate level:

$$a \succ b \succ c \succ a.$$

The collective preference may be complete, but it is not transitive. Therefore, it is not only the market exchange that is failing, as described in Chapter 1; so too is the vote.

This standard example can be easily generalized to a collective of q partners (a_1 to a_q). Imagine they are seated at a round table in their natural order, clockwise from a_1 to a_q. If we assume that each one places herself at the top of her preferences and places her $(q-1)$ partners in the order in which they fall running clockwise, then the electorate have the following (circular) preferences, which are complete and transitive:

$$(a_1): a_1 \succ a_2 \succ \ldots \succ a_{q-1} \succ a_q$$
$$(a_2): a_2 \succ a_3 \succ \ldots \succ a_q \succ a_1$$
$$\ldots$$
$$(a_q): a_q \succ a_1 \succ \ldots \succ a_{q-2} \succ a_{q-1}$$

---

[2] The introduction of this chapter is versioned for a political science audience in Crès (2018).
[3] The three pairs of candidates must be ranked; for example, partner a prefers a to b, b to c, and a to c: $a \succ b$, $b \succ c$, and $a \succ c$.
[4] For every (a, b, c), if $a \succ b$, and $b \succ c$, then $a \succ c$.

At the time of the vote, each one raises $(q-1)$ of the q votes against the person on her left-hand side. The collective preference generated by the majority vote is therefore cyclical:

$$a_1 \succ a_2 \succ \ldots \succ a_q \succ a_1.$$

The ubiquity of Condorcet cycles is the first and foremost challenge facing social choice theorists. For in theory, as Tullock (1981) wrote, "Without most improbable conditions, endless cycling would be expected. […] If we look at the real world, however, we observe not only is there no endless cycling, but acts are passed with reasonable dispatch and then remain unchanged for very long periods of time" (p. 189).

2.1.2 Super Majority: Arbitrating between Completeness and Transitivity

There is one simple way to ensure that the collective preference is no longer intransitive. This is to require a *super majority* when making collective choices. If a majority of more than two-thirds is needed to rank two candidates, then cycles of length three disappear; in order to break cycles of length q, the required super majority must be greater than $(q-1)/q$.

The use of a super majority can eliminate the intransitivity created by cycles. Unfortunately, there is a flip side to every coin. If the required majority is too high, then the collective preference becomes incomplete insofar as some pairs of candidates are no longer ranked by the collective entity. In the example with three partners, there is a majority of two out of three who vote for a over b, but that is not enough to validate the ranking $a \succ b$ at a collective level if the required majority is higher than 2/3.

The majority vote, whether qualified or not, is a simple and natural mechanism to *aggregate* individual preferences into a collective preference. But it is only partially successful, like trading on an imperfect or incomplete market. Individual preferences may be complete and transitive, but majority voting offers no guarantee that the collective preference will be.

A collective entity that wants to base its choices on the majority principle must therefore arbitrate between completeness and transitivity. To do this, it has a control variable: the required percentage for a majority to impose its choice. This variable ranges between 50 and 100 percent, between a simple majority and unanimity. The use of a simple majority (50 percent) guarantees a complete collective preference (provided there is not an even split).

Indeed, with individual preferences complete, there are only two possibilities: a majority in support of a over b, or a majority in support of b over a. The requirement of unanimity (100 percent) guarantees a transitive collective preference: if 100 percent of voters prefer a to b and b to c, then because the individual preferences are transitive, 100 percent of voters prefer a to c.

2.1.3 Collective Preference or Collective Choice?

A requirement of a complete and transitive collective preference is somewhat extreme. If one candidate naturally comes out on top, for example because she has a majority of votes over all the others (in which case she is called a *Condorcet winner*), then it matters little if cycles appear between the minority candidates. What is important is not so much the existence of a rational collective preference but rather the emergence of a *stable* collective choice. Stable here means one that is not defeated through majority voting by some other candidate.

Unfortunately, it is just as easy to illustrate the relative failure of the majority vote in accomplishing this task. Consider the simple matter of sharing profits between q selfish business partners. Whatever the initial distribution, there will always be a majority of $(q-1)$ partners who would prefer another distribution breakdown, whereby one partner would be expropriated and his share divided among the $(q-1)$ others. There is no such thing as a stable distribution; it is chaos. Unless, once again, a super majority of more than $(q-1)/q$ is required to impose a collective choice. But then every distribution is stable because each partner has a veto. This is the most extreme form of conservatism.

Here, too, arbitration is needed. Not between completeness and transitivity, but between chaos and conservatism. The cursor is again the percentage required for a super majority. The use of a simple majority guarantees protection against the conservatism of a minority, while a requirement of unanimity guarantees protection against chaos.

The central question is where to place the cursor. Every social choice problem is in fact characterized by a *stability threshold* of between 0 and 1, known as the *min-max* (Simpson, 1969; Kramer, 1972, 1973; see Section 2.5). When it comes to forging a collective preference, this threshold measures the tension between completeness and transitivity. It provides an indication of the extent to which the voting procedure must be conservative in order for a stable collective choice to be possible. In this regard, as schematic and provocative as it may seem, this threshold is a measure of just how flawed a democratic configuration is.

2.1.4 Stability Threshold: A Measure of Democratic Failings

The aggregation of circular individual preferences and the division of a cake are both examples of deceptive simplicity and clarity. It would be easy to lose sight of the fact that they are among the worst possible examples, those that push the dilemma of the social architect to its extreme, completeness and transitivity for the first, chaos and conservatism for the second. With regard to the former, the dilemma is extreme because to eliminate all possibilities of a cycle, the possibility of comparing two candidates must also be eliminated. In the case of the latter, it is extreme because there are only two possibilities: either everything is stable or nothing is. This dilemma is also extreme in theoretical terms because in both examples, the threshold for a super majority to ensure the acyclicity of the collective preference or the stability of the collective choice is $(q-1)/q$, a ratio which is higher than in the case of all other comparable social choice problems (Greenberg, 1979), whether they involve achieving an acyclical collective preference out of q candidates or a stable collective choice within a space of $(q-1)$ variables.[5] With a large number of stakeholders (high q value), this threshold is close to 1, i.e. approaching unanimity.

The versatility of the markets and the fluid behavior of individual market players are such that an even more extreme scenario is conceivable, one where the stability threshold equals 1: shareholders unanimously favor one candidate, say b, over the incumbent, candidate a; and reciprocally, shareholders unanimously favor candidate a over b, when a is the challenger and b is the incumbent; a Condorcet cycle (of length two) thus emerges:

$$a \succ b \succ a$$

which no majority rule can neutralize. This is a version of the well-known 'out with the old and in with the new,' based not on the reversal of individual preferences but that of the electorate: the fluidity of economic stakeholders and self-fulfilling prophecies can result in a situation in which the shareholders/voters

---

[5] In order to divide a cake, one must first establish what to allocate to $(q-1)$ individuals, whereby the last individual receives the residue. The dimension of this problem is therefore $(q-1)$.

are not the same when a or b is in charge. A description of this phenomenon is provided in Section 3.5.

There are also examples at the other end of the spectrum, where the stability threshold is close to 0. For example, in a unanimous collective entity in which everyone agrees about everything (as in a perfect market), the stability threshold equals 0: the candidate who gets all the votes will never be defeated, even if the required percentage is lower than a majority, indeed regardless of how low it is.

Are there cases midway between these two extremes, where the stability threshold is close to 0.5? The answer is yes. This happens when, for example, individual preferences are *single-peaked* (Black, 1948, 1958): if the collective choice problem relates to a single variable, for example the share of profits to reinvest in the firm, and if, furthermore, each individual shareholder has an ideal investment and the further the choice lies (upward or downward) from her ideal, the less satisfied this shareholder is, then the stability threshold equals 0.5. And it is the ideal investment of the median shareholder that is stable with a simple majority. Any alternative proposition will be rejected by a majority of shareholders. A higher investment will be rejected by the median shareholder and by all those who favor a lower investment—the definition of the median is such that they make up at least 50 percent of the electorate. Similarly, a lower investment will be rejected by the median shareholder and by all those who favor a higher investment. This is known as the *median voter theorem*, which will be further explored in Section 2.4. Section 2.5 will show that this result extends to collective choices relating simultaneously to several decision variables, and also that a stability threshold of 0.64 applies to a significant range of problems (Caplin & Nalebuff, 1988, 1991).

2.1.5 Economic Equilibrium and Political Stability

Management's choice of firm strategy raises authentic social choice problems. Let us briefly return to the approach adopted in Chapter 1, and consider at first that firms' production plans are fixed. Through the trading-driven alignment on the market, i.e. in a state of economic equilibrium according to Definition 1.4, each agent has an individual preference (in relation to the decisions made by firms) which is represented by his value vector. Therefore, each economic equilibrium carries its own stability threshold.

Let us assume that the firms' governance charters establish a rate (ρ) for a super majority when reaching decisions by vote. Only those economic equilibria with a stability threshold higher than ρ will be stable in political terms, hence giving rise to an *economic and political* equilibrium, named a ρ–*majority equilibrium*. It represents the stable states of the system (Definition 2.7). This is a notion of general equilibrium as in Definition 1.5, to the extent that production plans are equilibrium plans. This notion has three pillars: 1) the capacity of each agent to calculate an optimal consumption and investment plan based on her preferences; 2) free trade on the market leading to an economic equilibrium through the adjustment of prices; and 3) the impossibility, in a state of economic equilibrium, of finding an alternative to the status quo in each firm that would receive enough votes, i.e. a rate higher than ρ.

The crucial issue here is to choose the most judicious rate ρ for a super majority, as set out in the governance charter. The dilemma is always the same: if this rate equals 1, which means shareholder unanimity is required to change the status quo, then all economic equilibria are politically stable; if it equals zero, which means all changes, even if proposed by just one shareholder, are adopted, then no economic equilibrium is politically stable unless shareholders are all aligned. The judicious choice is to arbitrate as well as possible given this tension: between an overly conservative voting procedure that may end up protecting inefficient firm strategies, and an overly liberal procedure that may result in these strategies being too unstable. Intuitively, we can tell that a highly specific rate is hiding in the entrails of the model: the lowest ρ^* that can nonetheless guarantee the existence of at least one ρ^*–majority equilibrium. The aim of Chapter 3 is to seek out this ρ^*.

First, we must understand the geometry of our concept of political stability within the space of the value vectors. This is the focus of Sections 2.2 and 2.3, which express the principles of unanimity and majority in terms of relative positioning of these vectors. Sections 2.4 and 2.5 translate important results from social choice theory in the same terms, more appropriate to the neoclassical model of general equilibrium. Section 2.6 will conclude by explaining in which sense the stability of a political outcome is a matter of polarization of the electorate.

2.2 The Pareto Principle

The plan chosen by a firm is determined by the outcome of a political process of collective decision-making. The modelling presented in Chapter 1 enables us to analyze this political process by studying the relationships it establishes between the different value vectors.

Let $\mathcal{I}_j$ be the subset of consumers who participate in the decision-making process in firm j: in other words, its individual decision-makers (shareholders and possibly other stakeholders, i.e. agents affected by the firm's decisions— disregarding agency problems: the management does what the electorate decides to do). Whatever the political process, ultimately a production plan y_j is chosen. Lemma 1.1 tells us that this plan is supported by value vector ∇_j. The fundamental hypothesis is that the political process is democratic in nature to the extent that ∇_j, one way or another, reflects the preferences of the individual decision-makers. The value vectors $(\nabla_i)_{i \in \mathcal{I}_j}$ of the individual decision-makers are said to be *aggregated* to form the firm's value vector ∇_j.

Beyond asserting the democratic principle, what else can be said about the aggregation process? One minimal hypothesis is that of the unanimity rule: assuming that if within a collective entity all individual members prefer plan y' to plan y, then the entity as a whole must respect this unanimity and also prefer plan y' to plan y.

2.2.1 The Pareto Principle: (Strong) Unanimity Principle

A strong version of this hypothesis is the Pareto principle: if all members (weakly) prefer y' to y, and at least one member strictly prefers y' to y, then the collective must also strictly prefer y' to y.

The following definition establishes the Pareto principle for value vectors.

Definition 2.1 *Let* $\left((\nabla_i)_{i \in \mathcal{I}}, (\nabla_j)_{i \in \mathcal{J}} \right)$ *be value vectors.*

- ∇_j *respects the Pareto principle if for all* $\Delta y \in \mathbb{R}^\ell$,
  $\nabla_i \cdot \Delta y \geq 0 \, \forall i \in \mathcal{I}_j$ *with at least one strict inequality* $\implies \nabla_j \cdot \Delta y > 0$.
- $(\nabla_j)_{j \in \mathcal{J}}$ *is* Pareto stable *if* ∇_j *respects the Pareto principle for every j.*

The unanimity rule is perhaps the most common possible hypothesis in relation to an aggregation mechanism. It is a founding hypothesis in the literature on the aggregation of individual preferences, in particular underpinning Arrow's theorem (1951). It is also a building block of welfare economics, in particular the literature on the joint aggregation of beliefs and tastes, starting with Harsanyi's (1955) social aggregation theorem, extended to Savage's framework by Hylland & Zeckhauser (1979) and Mongin (1995), and to the case of multiple priors by Crès et al. (2011), among others. Under another form, it appears as a classical assumption of the literature on the aggregation of judgments (Kornhauser & Sager, 1986; List & Pettit, 2002)—a.k.a. logical aggregation theory (Mongin, 2012).

Interestingly, the standard argument for profit maximization (on a perfect and complete market) already stems from a simple form of the unanimity rule: all shareholder agree on maximizing their own respective income, therefore they unanimously vote for profit maximization, hence firms *should* implement a profit-maximizing production plan. In some sense, this essay provides a generalization of this argument to settings with market failures.

The unanimity rule is arguably a mild requirement. It ensures that the group does not take decisions at odds with the interest of *all* its members. In the context of aggregating individual preferences, it implies nothing if at the outset there is not unanimity between the different group members, which is what makes it minimal. In the context of Arrovian aggregation, it is the least controversial axiom—at least in comparison with the independence axiom. It is compatible with most aggregation mechanisms that come to mind, beginning with voting procedures of all types.

The same can be said of the Pareto principle, which is an amended version of the unanimity rule.[6] Although mild, this principle has a strong consequence for the positioning of ∇_j with respect to $(\nabla_i)_{i \in \mathcal{I}}$. Let the convex cone of $(\nabla_i)_{i \in \mathcal{I}}$ be:

$$\angle(\nabla_i)_{i \in \mathcal{I}} = \left\{ \nabla \mid \exists (\mu_i)_{i \in \mathcal{I}} \in \mathbb{R}_+^{|\mathcal{I}|} \text{ such that } \nabla = \sum_{i \in \mathcal{I}} \mu_i \nabla_i \right\},$$

and let $\angle^+(\nabla_i)_{i \in \mathcal{I}}$ denote the positive cone, i.e. such that $\mu_i > 0$ for every $i \in \mathcal{I}$.

The Pareto principle implies that the value vector that supports the chosen plan is in the positive cone of the decision-makers' value vectors.

Proposition 2.1 *Let* $((\nabla_i)_{i \in \mathcal{I}}, (\nabla_j)_{j \in \mathcal{J}})$ *be value vectors.* ∇_j *respects the Pareto principle if and only if* $\nabla_j \in \angle^+(\nabla_i)_{i \in \mathcal{I}_j}$.

∇_j is therefore a weighted sum of the individual decision-makers' value vectors; it is an average of these vectors if they are normalized. In the second part of this essay, we will look in more detail at how to interpret this proposition. In brief, the first interpretation is statistical: while the individual value vectors $(\nabla_i)_{i \in \mathcal{I}}$ are necessarily biased by individual subjectivity, this is

---

[6] In the logical aggregation literature, the strength of the Pareto principle has been extensively discussed: see, for instance, Nehring (2005), Mongin (2008) and Nehring et al. (2016).

eliminated *on average* in vector ∇_j, which therefore expresses more a *judgment* than an opinion or a preference. The second interpretation is geometric: the cone $\angle^+(\nabla_i)_{i \in I}$ delimits the space of individual opinions or preferences; what Proposition 2.1 asserts is that respect for the Pareto principle means the firm is unable to free itself from these limits. If $\angle^+$ is the 'box' of individual opinions, then the firm cannot think outside the box.

Can more be said about the location of the value vector within $\angle^+$? The answer is yes, when the political process authorizes individual decision-makers to be paid in exchange for their support for changes to the production plan.

2.2.2 The Pareto Principle with Transfers

If this is the case, we can intuitively understand that some plans which were once stable now cease to be. Assume there are two decision-makers, i and i', and that for a particular change Δy, i loses w and i' gains w'. If $w' > w$, then i' could compensate i so that both of them benefit from the change. The possibility of such transfers implies that one and only one value vector within $\angle^+(\nabla_i)_{i \in I}$ supports a stable decision, as stated in Proposition 2.2.

Let us amend the Pareto principle to take such transfers into account. Let $(w_i)_{i \in I_j}$ be transfers, where $w_i \in \mathbb{R}$ is the payment received by $i \in I_j$; they are *sustainable* (in accounting terms) if $\sum_{i \in I_j} w_i \leq 0$.

Definition 2.2 *Let $((\nabla_i)_{i \in I}, (\nabla_j)_{j \in J})$ be value vectors. ∇_j respects the Pareto principle with transfers if for all $\Delta y \in \mathbb{R}^\ell$ and for all sustainable transfers $(w_i)_{i \in I_j}$,*

$$\nabla_i \cdot \Delta y + w_i \geq 0 \; \forall i \in I_j \text{ with at least one strict inequality} \implies \nabla_j \cdot \Delta y > 0.$$

The Pareto principle with transfers implies that the value vector that supports the chosen plan is a very special one element of $\angle^+$, i.e. the one for which each agent carries the same weight: $\mu_i = 1$ for every i.

Proposition 2.2 *Let $((\nabla_i)_{i \in I}, (\nabla_j)_{j \in J})$ be value vectors. ∇_j respects the Pareto principle with transfers if and only if ∇_j is collinear to $\sum_{i \in I_j} \nabla_i$.*

Authorizing transfers between individual decision-makers so they can offer their support in exchange for certain changes in production in practice amounts to creating new markets that can internalize externalities. If these transfers are themselves protected from information asymmetries (which is doubtful given that one's willingness to pay for a change in production is private information which it is not in the interest of the individual to reveal), then they effectively correct the failure of the market, and it is no surprise that in the next chapter we will see that they restore the allocative efficiency of transactions as much as could be reasonably hoped for.

Before turning toward the majority principle, let us briefly show why respect of the Pareto principle by the ∇_j implies stability of production.

2.2.3 Stability of Production Plans

We'll say that plan $y_j \in \partial \mathcal{Y}_j$ is Pareto stable (in short) if there is no other plan $y_j' \in \mathcal{Y}_j$ which is considered at least as good as y_j by all decision-makers, and strictly better by at least one of them.

Definition 2.3 *Plan $y_j \in \partial \mathcal{Y}_j$ is Pareto stable if there does not exist $y_j' \in \mathcal{Y}_j$ such that $\nabla_i \cdot y_j' \geq \nabla_i \cdot y_j$ for every $i \in \mathcal{I}_j$, with at least one strict inequality.*

As illustrated by Fig. 1.1, if ∇_j supports $y_j \in \partial \mathcal{Y}_j$, all $y_j' \in \mathcal{Y}_j$ different from y_j will be such that $\nabla_j \cdot (y_j' - y_j) < 0$, because of the convexity of $\mathcal{Y}_j$; which immediately yields the following lemma.

Lemma 2.1 *If $\nabla_j(y_j)$ respects the Pareto principle, then plan $y_j \in \partial \mathcal{Y}_j$ is Pareto stable.*

Let us now turn toward the notion of stability with respect to the majority principle.

2.3 The Majority Principle

The perspective adopted in this section is that the decisions made by firms should reflect the will of a majority of individual decision-makers.

2.3.1 Voting Weights

The ownership of firms is determined by shares $(\theta_i)_{i \in \mathcal{I}}$. Their governance is based on the majority principle and depends on the voting weights of each consumer in each firm: $\lambda = (\lambda_{ij})_{i \in \mathcal{I}, j \in \mathcal{J}} \in \mathbb{R}_+^{IJ}$, where $\sum_{i \in \mathcal{I}} \lambda_{ij} = 1$ for every j.

Governance may or may not be linked to ownership. When voting weights are not linked to ownership, we face *stakeholder governance*. Stakeholders are the agents affected one way or another by the firm's decisions, regardless of whether or not they hold shares in the firm. In general equilibrium, generically all agents are stakeholders.

Governance can be more or less democratic, depending on whether a census suffrage system is used, i.e. whether one's voting weight depends on the number of shares held. This essay considers two main forms of governance.

Definition 2.4 *Shareholder governance (one share, one vote) is defined as:* $\lambda_{ij} = \max\{0, \theta_{ij}\}$; *and stakeholder democracy (one person, one vote) as:* $\lambda_{ij} = 1/I$.

2.3.2 The ρ–majority Principle

The value vectors $(\nabla_i)_{i\in I_j}$ of the individual decision-makers in firm j are aggregated to form value vector ∇_j. Let $\rho \in [0, 1[$ be the required rate for a super majority to reach decisions.

For change Δy, let $\lambda_j(\Delta y)$ be the aggregate voting weight of the set of consumers in favor of the change.

Definition 2.5 *Let* $((\nabla_i)_{i\in I}, (\nabla_j)_{j\in J})$ *be value vectors.*

- ∇_j *respects the ρ–majority principle if for all* $\Delta y \in \mathbb{R}^\ell$, $\lambda_j(\Delta y) > \rho$ *implies* $\nabla_j \cdot \Delta y > 0$.
- $(\nabla_j)_{j\in J}$ *is stable with respect to the ρ–majority principle (ρ–stable in short) if* ∇_j *respects the ρ–majority principle for every j.*

As for Pareto stability, the definition of ρ–stability naturally extends to production plans.

Definition 2.6 *Plan* $y_j \in \partial \mathcal{Y}_j$ *is ρ–stable if there does not exist* $y'_j \in \mathcal{Y}_j$ *such that* $\lambda_j(y'_j - y_j) > \rho$.

A counterpart of Lemma 2.1 easily follows.

Lemma 2.2 *If* $\nabla_j(y_j)$ *respects the ρ–majority principle, then plan* $y_j \in \partial \mathcal{Y}_j$ *is ρ–stable.*

We will now look at some useful figures with which to understand the geometric properties of political stability.

2.3.3 Geometry of Political Stability

In the case of a single firm, the two figures below show different distributions of individual value vectors in an economy where $\ell = 3, I = 5$ and voting weights are equal. All value vectors are normalized such that they can be represented by points on a plane, and (vector) ∇ is in the cone defined by (∇_i) when in the figure (point) ∇ is contained within the convex hull of (∇_i).

Fig. 2.2 represents an unfavorable configuration: ∇ is not contained within the convex hull of the $(\nabla_i)_{i \in \mathcal{M}}$, where $\mathcal{M} = \{2, 3, 4, 5\}$. There is therefore a marginal change in plan (orthogonal to the dotted vertical line pointing to the right) which receives the 4 votes of $\mathcal{M}$ against the status quo supported by ∇. In this case, the stability of ∇ requires a super majority of 80 percent or more.

Fig. 2.1 represents a more favorable configuration. Here, the size of the largest groups for which ∇ is not contained within the convex hull of $(\nabla_i)_{i \in \mathcal{M}}$ is 3: $\{1, 2, 3\}$, $\{2, 3, 4\}$, $\{3, 4, 5\}$, $\{4, 5, 1\}$, $\{5, 1, 2\}$. In the political game, this means that every change divides the voting population into two groups, one sized 2 and one sized 3, as indicated in the five dotted lines—one for each possible division, corresponding to each of the five previous groups. In this case, ∇ is stable with a super majority of 60 percent or more.

Based on what these figures point to intuitively, it is possible to propose a description of ρ−stable value vectors. Let us say that a coalition $\mathcal{M}$ of individuals is *decisive* with a super majority at rate ρ if its aggregate voting weight is greater than ρ: $\lambda_j(\mathcal{M}) > \rho$. Let $\mathcal{D}_j^\rho \subset 2^{\{1, \dots, I\}}$ be the set of decisive majorities in firm j. The following holds as an immediate corollary of Proposition 2.1.

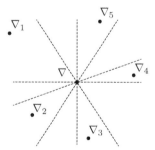

Fig. 2.1 A 0.6-stable configuration

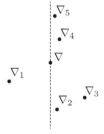

Fig. 2.2 A 0.8-stable configuration

Proposition 2.3 *Let* $((\nabla_i)_{i \in I}, (\nabla_j)_{j \in J})$ *be value vectors.* ∇_j *respects the* ρ*–majority principle if and only if it is contained within the intersection of the positive cones of the value vectors for all decisive majorities:*

$$\nabla_j \in \bigcap_{M \in \mathcal{D}_j^\rho} \angle^+ (\nabla_i)_{i \in M}$$

We will now return to Fig. 2.1 and let $\rho = 0.6$. The decisive coalitions comprise four individuals and there are five such coalitions, depending on the individual excluded. All ∇ in the intersection of the convex hulls of the value vectors for these five coalitions are 0.6–stable. This corresponds to a ∇ included in the inner pentagon in Fig. 2.3.

2.3.4 ρ–majority Equilibrium

A central notion of equilibrium used in this essay stems from Definition 1.4. This is a notion of general equilibrium as in Definition 1.5, to the extent that production plans are equilibrium plans. But this notion of equilibrium for plans is a political notion (plans are stable with respect to the majority principle), and not based on value maximization.

Definition 2.7 *A* ρ*–majority equilibrium* (p^*, x^*, y^*) *is an equilibrium such that value vectors* $(\nabla_j^*)_{j \in J}$ *supporting* y^* *are* ρ*–stable.*

When unanimity is required to change the status quo,[7] there is only one decisive coalition—that of all individual decision-makers—and Proposition 2.3

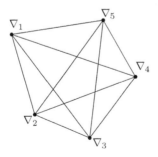

Fig. 2.3 The 0.6-stable set

---

[7] The case of unanimity is represented here with a certain liberty in the notation by $\rho = 1^-$, with the convention $\lambda(\mathcal{M}) > 1^- \iff \lambda(\mathcal{M}) \geq 1$; then Pareto stability and ρ-stability are one and the same.

boils down to Proposition 2.1. This corresponds to a cone of value vectors with maximum extension, and many production plans are stable. As ρ decreases, not only does the size of the cones of decisive coalitions also decrease (as the size of the decisive coalitions decreases), so too does the size of their intersection (as the number of decisive coalitions increases). This produces a scissors effect.

Intuitively, this scissors effect can be thought to reduce the scope of the set of stable production plans. This intuition is to some extent confirmed by the marginal case of $\rho = 0.5$, which has a peculiar property: at a 0.5–majority equilibrium, there is only one stable production plan in the firm; furthermore, it is the best plan for a particular individual who, one might say, becomes the virtual decision-maker. We will see this in the next section.

2.4 Simple Majority

We have long known that outside of single-peaked preferences (Black, 1948), and in particular when the plans being determined by voters are multidimensional, there is generally no equilibrium with a simple majority (Plott, 1967). It is nonetheless interesting to study the properties of such equilibria *when they occur*. These properties are remarkable. Not only does everything take place as if the decision-making power were in the hands of a given individual, but in the case of shareholder governance this individual is easy to identify; it is the person with the biggest shareholding in the firm.

The results in this section are borrowed from DeMarzo (1993). The stability concept in this article is slightly different from ours: value vectors $(\nabla_j)_{j \in \mathcal{J}}$ are stable with respect to simple majority when the inequalities in Definitions 2.5 and 2.6 are weak, i.e. if there is no alternative that gets *at least* half of votes against the status quo. With some peotic license, we'll write that the corresponding equilibrium is a 0.5^-–majority equilibrium.

2.4.1 A Decision-Maker in the Shadows

At a 0.5^-–majority equilibrium, in every firm the plan is a solution for the value vector of a particular agent.

Proposition 2.4 *(DeMarzo, 1993) At a 0.5^-–majority equilibrium, in every firm j, there is an agent $i(j)$ such that $\nabla_j^* = \nabla_{i(j)}^*$.*

In a unidimensional scenario, where the (∇_i) are distributed along a line, $i(j)$ is the *median* agent; this is the agent whose value vector is at the median of the distribution of the individual value vectors. But in a multidimensional scenario, who is the decision-maker operating in the shadows?

2.4.2 The Dominant Shareholder

Under the condition that each triplet of value vectors is independent (a property named hereafter as '3–independence'[8]), the decision-maker in the shadows is none other than the shareholder with the largest voting weight. Under a shareholder governance system (one share, one vote), it is the shareholder with the largest share in the firm.

Proposition 2.5 *(DeMarzo, 1993) At a 0.5^-–majority equilibrium, under the condition of 3–independence, the decision-maker in the shadows is the dominant voter: $\lambda_{i(j)} \geq \lambda_i$ for all $i \neq i(j)$.*

In a multidimensional scenario, the presence of 0.5^-–majority equilibria is unfortunately the exception rather than the rule. This usually requires a super majority at a rate of between $\rho = 0.5$ and $\rho = 1^-$, i.e. between a simple majority and unanimity.

But what is this rate? Proposition 2.3 clearly suggests that if the required rate for a super majority is too high, then far too many production plans are stable and the majority rule is too conservative. If, in contrast, the rate is too low, then there is no equilibrium and nothing is stable, leading to chaos. Following that logical path, the right rate ρ^* is the lowest that can nonetheless guarantee the existence of at least one ρ^*–majority equilibrium. The aim of the next section is to seek out this rate, while at the same time reviewing some of the results thrown up by social choice theory.

2.5 Stability Threshold

Broadly speaking, ρ–majority equilibria are non-existent where $\rho = 0.5$, and they are too numerous and indeterminate where $\rho = 1^-$. So for each economy there is a threshold above which there is a majority equilibrium

---

[8] This condition generally hods in a multidimensional scenario with a sufficient number of missing markets. Naturally, it does not hold in a unidimensional, or even bidimensional, space.

and below which there is not. This is the notion of the stability threshold of each economy, presented in the introduction to this chapter. It is natural to consider this threshold as the optimal rate for a super majority as set out in the governance charter; optimal insofar as it arbitrates with precision between chaos and conservatism.

Two reasons come to mind to argue against a rate higher than ρ^*. First, it would cause too much indeterminacy in the economy, making it more difficult to achieve coordination between agents. Second, it would excessively protect the status quo, allowing a poor management team to remain entrenched behind this protection. But there is a third reason, which we will look at in the next chapter: ρ^*—majority equilibria offer reasonable guarantees of efficiency in economic terms.

Some political scientists look favorably on the absence of political equilibria, as this paves the way for deliberation and the construction of a more consensual society (McGann, 2006). This is an interesting point of view, and one we will return to in detail in the second part of this essay. It can however be pointed out that investment decisions require long-term visibility, which is an argument in favor of at least minimum levels of stability in firm decisions.

Unfortunately, as illustrated by the discussion of Condorcet cycles and the sharing of profits at the beginning of this chapter, the existence of an equilibrium may require a very high super majority rate.

2.5.1 Median (Multivariate) Voter: Threshold of $1 - 1/\ell$

For the purposes of simplification, let us assume that each agent i has a preference within the set of the firm's production plans $\mathcal{Y}$. This preference can be represented by the correspondence $\mathcal{P}_i : \mathcal{Y} \longrightarrow \mathcal{Y}$, where $y' \in \mathcal{P}_i(y)$ means that agent i prefers y' to y, where y is the status quo.[9] In the simple framework of Chapter 1, it can be represented by value vector ∇_i such that $\mathcal{P}_i(y) \subset \{y' \mid \nabla_i \cdot y' > \nabla_i \cdot y\}$.

Let $\mathcal{I}(y, y')$ denote the set of agents who prefer y' to y:

$$\mathcal{I}(y, y') = \{i \mid y' \in \mathcal{P}_i(y)\}.$$

The aggregate preference is represented by the correspondence $\mathcal{P}^\rho : \mathcal{Y} \longrightarrow \mathcal{Y}$, where $y' \in \mathcal{P}^\rho(y)$ if and only if $\#\mathcal{I}(y, y') > \rho I$.

---

[9] These preferences can be incomplete and/or intransitive; in particular, it is possible to have $y' \in \mathcal{P}_i(y)$ when y is the status quo, and $y \in \mathcal{P}_i(y')$ when y' is the status quo.

An immediate generalization of the problem of sharing profits (or dividing a cake) reveals that a rate of $1 - 1/\ell$ is a *lower bound* for the stability threshold.

Proposition 2.6 *If $\rho < 1 - 1/\ell$, there are value vectors $(\nabla_i)_{i \in \mathcal{I}}$ such that there is no ρ-majority equilibrium.*

The following result reveals that the problem of dividing a cake is the worst scenario, in that a rate of $1 - 1/\ell$ is also an *upper bound* for the stability threshold.

Theorem 2.1 *(Greenberg, 1979) Assume*

- *Continuity: $\forall i \in I$, $\mathcal{P}_i$ has an open graph in $\mathcal{Y} \times \mathcal{Y}$.*
- *Convexity: $\forall i \in I$, and $\forall y \in \mathcal{Y}$, $y \notin co(\mathcal{P}_i(y))$ — where $co(X)$ denotes the convex hull of X.*

Then if $\rho \geq 1 - 1/\ell$ there exists a ρ-majority equilibrium.

This result applies to our model based on value vectors independently of their distribution. It depends only on the number of conflict dimensions, in our case $\ell - 1$. The bad news is that this threshold is close to unanimity as soon as the number of conflict dimensions rises. The complexity of economic affairs is such that decisions relating to production plans involve at least four or five dimensions of choice, in which cases the stability threshold suggested by Greenberg's theorem is 75 or 80 percent. In order to obtain equilibria with lower super majorities, additional hypotheses must be made in relation to the distribution of the value vectors.

2.5.2 Mean (Multivariate) Voter: Threshold of 64 percent

Caplin & Nalebuff (1988, 1991) propose a fruitful approach. Consider the rate for a super majority

$$\rho(c) = 1 - \left(\frac{c}{c+1}\right)^c.$$

The rate $\rho(c)$ increases with c towards $1 - 1/e \approx 0.632$. The authors indicate the conditions under which there is a $\rho(c)$-majority equilibrium, and therefore a 0.64-majority equilibrium. Contrary to Greenberg's theorem, this result is valid regardless of the number of conflict dimensions.

The original result is formulated in a version of this model with a continuum of consumers. Their preferences in relation to the plans vary in accordance with n continuous parameters $\iota \in \mathbb{R}^n$, contained in a convex support $\mathcal{I}$, where each ι represents a type of agent. Type ι preferences are represented by a continuous utility function $V(\iota, y)$, and the distribution of the different types within the firm is represented over $\mathcal{I}$ by a probability measure with density φ.

Let us define the mean voter as being type $\mathring{\iota}$, located at the center of gravity of the distribution of the ι:

$$\mathring{\iota}_k = \int_{\mathcal{I}} \iota_k \varphi(\iota) d\iota, \text{ for every } k, 1 \leq k \leq n,$$

and let $\mathring{y}$ be the best production plan for $\mathring{\iota}$.

Let us assume that the preferences are linear in $\mathcal{I}$:

$$V(\iota, y) = v_0(y) + \sum_{k=1}^{n} \iota_k v_k(y),$$

where $V : \mathbb{R}^n \times \mathcal{Y} \to \mathbb{R}$ and $v_k : \mathcal{Y} \to \mathbb{R}$ for every $k, 1 \leq k \leq n$.

Let us further assume that the density function φ is σ-concave on the support $\mathcal{I}$, in that f^σ is concave: for all $\iota, \iota' \in \mathcal{I}$, for all $t \in [0, 1]$,

$$\varphi((1-t)\iota + t\iota') \geq ((1-t)\varphi(\iota)^\sigma + t\varphi(\iota')^\sigma)^{1/\sigma}.$$

Theorem 2.2 (*Caplin & Nalebuff, 1991*) *If* $\sigma \geq -1/(n+1)$, *then* $\mathring{y}$ *is a* $\rho(n + 1/\sigma)$-*majority equilibrium.*

We can use images for a simple depiction of the political game: two opponents must share an (electoral) cake, represented by support $\mathcal{I}$ with a σ-concave distribution. The first player indicates a spot on the cake and the second must cut it in two in a straight line at that spot and choose the portion she wants. The first player's spot represents the status quo and the second player's cut the competing production plan to alter the status quo. The fact that the second player cuts the cake in a straight line is a result of the principle of minimum differentiation: it is in the challenger's interest to suggest only an infinitesimal deviation from the status quo (orthogonal to the dividing line).

Of course, the second player is intent on cutting the cake into the two most unequal portions possible so that her portion is as big as possible. This size is the *score* of the status quo. The first player therefore endeavors to indicate the point with the lowest score, so that the portion given to his opponent is as small as possible. This size is known as the Simpson–Kramer *min–max*.

Theorem 2.2 establishes that the center of gravity of the distribution of the value vectors is a good approximation of the first player's optimal choice. And its score is lower than $\rho(c)$. This is due to the fact that no hyperplane divides a compact and convex support with an σ-concave distribution across its center of gravity in such a way that one of the two portions contains more than $100\rho(c)$ percent of the total weight.

Theorem 2.2 has a counterpart for discrete and finite populations (see Caplin & Nalebuff, 1988, Theorem 3) that is better suited to the framework of this essay.

Proposition 2.7 *If the agent types (a finite number) are drawn independently using a σ-concave distribution, then as the population increases the min–max ratio almost certainly converges towards its limit value.*

A stability threshold of around 64 percent is closer to the norm in this regard. The French and American constitutions can be amended with respective majorities of 60 and 66 percent; for the European Union, the Maastricht treaty had established a norm at 72 percent, and the draft Constitutional Treaty had proposed a mix of 65 percent (of the states) and 55 percent (of the population). Yet this is still quite high; can we do better?

2.5.3 When Chance Gets Involved: Threshold of 50 percent

The distribution of the value vectors is crucial. If it is symmetrical, then the center of symmetry is stable with respect to a simple majority (see Tullock, 1967; Grandmont, 1978) and the stability threshold is 50 percent. Ultimately this is the best possible configuration. But how hopeful can we be that such a configuration will present itself?

From a geometric perspective, if we consider a spatial voting model with dimension ℓ and involving I voters, we are looking at a distribution of I (random) points in $\mathbb{R}^\ell$. Some 'natural' distributions of random points have been suggested by stochastic geometry (see Schneider, 2004). Among these distributions, the following plays a central role: each configuration of $I > \ell$ points in general position in $\mathbb{R}^\ell$ is affinely equivalent to the orthogonal projection of the vertices of a spherico-regular simplex with I vertices onto a linear sub-space of dimension ℓ. This construct establishes a bijective correspondence between the affine equivalence classes (preserving orientation) of such configurations of random points and the Grassmanian $G(I, \ell)$ of the (oriented) sub-spaces with dimension ℓ in $\mathbb{R}^I$.

The so-called *Grassmann approach* considers the probability distribution on the set of affine equivalence classes of I-tuples in general position in $\mathbb{R}^\ell$ that stems from the unique rotation-invariant probability measure on $G(I, \ell)$— known as the Haar probability measure—which intuitively selects 'with equal probability' the oriented ℓ-spaces on which the simplex is projected. Based on an observation made by Affentranger & Schneider (1992), Baryshnikov & Vitale (1994) showed that by adopting this Grassman approach, *the resulting point set coincides in distribution with a standard Gaussian sample.*

What is surprising about this approach is that it transforms the worst-case configuration, that of the division of a cake in which the value vectors ∇_i are the vertices of a simplex, into an ideal configuration in stochastic terms, where the value vectors ∇_i are distributed according to a standard Gaussian law, and therefore distributed symmetrically (Crès & Ünver, 2010).

2.6 A Matter of Polarization

The theorems of Greenberg and Caplin & Nalebuff are oases in the desolate terrain of social choice theory. They are among the few results, based on a deterministic perspective, identifying situations with general scope in which aggregation is possible. The Grassmann approach, on the other hand, is based on a stochastic perspective. The only hope it offers is that the worst outcome is never certain.[10] Another strength of the theorems of Greenberg and Caplin & Nalebuff is that they reveal why dividing a cake is the worst of all possible social choice scenarios. This is mainly due to the fact that individual preferences are polarized to the extreme—both in dimension and in distribution.

Preferences are polarized in dimension insofar as each agent opens up a dimension of conflict by adding a decision variable: his own share of the money.[11] Should the distribution of the money increase this share, or instead favor the aggregate shares of the other agents? This situation is very different

---

[10] In the same vein, one finds an abundant literature on the probability that Condorcet cycles appear, initiated by Guilbaud (1952). Computations (e.g. DeMeyer & Plott, 1970; Gehrlein & Fishburn, 1976) show that under the assumption of *impartial culture* the probability of a Condorcet cycle for the simple majority rule can be relatively low. But it increases with the number of alternatives and voters, and tends toward 1 for big numbers. More optimistic, Balasko & Crès (1997) demonstrate (under a slightly different assumption) that cycles are rare beyond a super majority of 53 percent, independently of the number of alternatives and voters. See also Balasko & Crès (1998) and Crès (2001).

[11] See footnote 5. If there are q shareholders, the dimension of the conflict space is $(q - 1)$.

in the case of collective decisions relating to a fixed and limited number of public choices. For example, if it is a matter of choosing what share of profits to reinvest, then the conflict space is unidimensional regardless of the number of agents.

Preferences are polarized in distribution insofar as each agent is only worried about his own share of the money and has no concerns for those of his fellow agents. Worse still, each agent is the only one who wants to increase his own share: all the others are against such an increase as it would be to their detriment. This makes the preferences *extremist*. And to top it off the voting weights (one person, one vote) are uniformly distributed over each of these extremes.[12]

The degrees to which individual preferences are polarized in dimension and in distribution within a collective entity are crucial parameters for assessing the homogeneity of an electorate. Intuition suggests that the greater the number of conflict dimensions (the variables on which the collective must simultaneously vote), the more the electorate is potentially heterogeneous. Such heterogeneity intensifies as voters have individual preferences representing an increasing number of extremist opinions within this conflict space. Intuition also suggests that the more the electorate is uniformly distributed over these extremist preferences, the more heterogeneous it will be. Lastly, the more the electorate is heterogeneous, the more the majority vote fails. The theorems of Greenberg and Caplin & Nalebuff therefore provide ways to measure the extent of the failure of democracy in the firm.

Chapter 3 shows *how trading on the market attenuates the polarization in dimension and distribution of electorates* formed at GAs, thereby assisting the majority principle. It also shows *how the majority principle promotes economic efficiency*, and in so doing mitigates the failure of the market. It is the key chapter in Part I of this essay, illustrating the alliance between trading and voting when it comes to stable and efficient decisions. It is a resolutely optimistic chapter but does not overlook the limitations and fragility of this alliance.

---

[12] One also finds extremely polarized individual preferences in Condorcet's example, described in the introduction. First of all, they are polarized with regard to the cycle:

$$a_1 \succ a_2 \succ \ldots \succ a_q \succ a_1$$

which is based on the q rankings of pairs $a_i \succ a_{i+1}$, where i varies from 1 to q (with the convention $a_{q+1} = a_1$). Each of the q individual preferences is aligned with exactly $(q - 1)$ of these q pair rankings; this is the maximum before the individual preference itself becomes cyclical, which is ruled out. These q individual preferences are therefore exactly the q preferences most in sync with the cycle, in respect of which they are also extremist preferences. Furthermore, their distribution is polarized as, once again, the voting weights are uniformly distributed over each of these extremes.

3

Voting and Trading in Symbiosis

3.1 Democracy and the Market: A Perfect Match?

We will now return to the case of a group of shareholders choosing a production plan. In the world of social choice, this problem has a particular feature that distinguishes it in one crucial way from more classical scenarios: its parameters—the identity of the shareholders, their preferences, and their respective weights in the collective decision—are not determined exogenously but instead by trading on the market. Shareholders at a GA do not represent an electorate brought together at a particular point in time by the random circumstances of their birth. One becomes a shareholder by choice. And if economic theory has one thing to say about the preferences of shareholders, it is that even though they may have their share of subjectivity, they are determined not by any external ideology, whether inherited or acquired, but by the need to satisfy consumption and investment needs. The individual preference of a shareholder, summed up in his value vector, depends on the equilibrium attained.

The parameters of this social choice problem are therefore endogenous. Not only the electorate, but also the preferences of its voters and potentially their respective weights in the voting procedure, are all the product of the interaction between agents on the market.[1] They are determined in accordance with the principle of consensual transactions between rational agents. This raises the following question: does this market mechanism—our invisible hand operating upstream of collective decisions—facilitate the majority voting procedure? In other words, does the market lend a helping hand to democracy?

---

[1] A parallel can be identified with the model used by Tiebout (1956) for the provision of local public goods. Local governments (here: companies) offer bundles of public services (here: production plans) at different fiscal rates (here: asset prices). Citizens move from one location to another (here: investors adjust their portfolios) according to their preferences and fiscal rates, and an equilibrium is reached. The electorate in each location is therefore determined endogenously by fiscal competition. There is one difference, however: it is possible for an investor to become a 'citizen' in several companies at once by developing a diversified portfolio of assets, a bit like people who own several homes for the purposes of fiscal optimization.

Democracy, the Market, and the Firm: How the Interplay between Trading and Voting Fosters Political Stability and Economic Efficiency. Hervé Crès and Mich Tvede, Oxford University Press. © Hervé Crès and Mich Tvede 2021.
DOI: 10.1093/oso/9780192894731.003.0004

3.1.1 The Market Supporting Democracy in the Firm

This question, spectaculary illustrated by the unanimity displayed at share-holders' assemblies, can be rephrased: are the collective entities which emerge endogenously on the market less conflictual than others?

We know that if the market is perfect, then the theory gives us a direct response in the affirmative, a resounding and definitive yes. For in the absence of a market, value vectors are calculated based on the consumers' initial endowments; it is easy to show that for almost all of these endowments the value vectors point in every possible direction; in other words, the level of conflict is at its maximum. Now consider a perfect market: at equilibrium, these value vectors all become identical as if by magic, i.e. the level of conflict is at its minimum. The perfect market does more than lend a helping hand to democracy: it swoops to its rescue and saves it from chaos.

But if the market is imperfect, or incomplete, what remains of this alignment?

In the case of an incomplete market, Theorem 3.2 provides a response to this question: partial alignment nonetheless occurs because the conflicts are elimi-nated in any space in which financial transfers are possible. At equilibrium, all that is left is a residual number of conflict dimensions to match the missing financial assets. Therefore, the less the market is incomplete, the fewer the number of conflict dimensions at equilibrium, and the less the preferences of shareholders display dimensional polarization. Greenberg's theorem translates this as follows: the more the market makes it possible to resolve conflicts over values between shareholders, the less it is necessary to give veto power to minorities in order to secure stability. So yes, unequivocally, the market lends a helping hand to democracy and protects it from the worst outcomes.

And that's not all. Consumers buy shares in those firms that best satisfy their consumption, insurance, and investment needs. And with equal wealth, the number of shares they buy increases as a firm better satisfies these needs. An electorate made up of shareholders is therefore subject to two self-selection mechanisms: the identity of the voters and their individual electoral weight in the voting procedure when each share carries one vote. These mechanisms therefore tend to bring together consumers with shared opinions and needs. Their opinions are linked to their preferences and beliefs: where and when, in space and time, does the consumer prefer to hold resources? What are the chances that he will find himself in that place at that time? Their needs are linked (to their preferences and) to their endowments: what initial resources would they have in that place and at that time ? Intuition tells us that these self-selection mechanisms bring together voters with less discordant opinions and more similar needs than if they were put together randomly. It is therefore reasonable to expect that the value vectors of a group of shareholders from the same firm will display less distributional polarization than in the economy as a whole. Proposition 3.4 points to conclusive results in this regard.

In the presence of direct or pecuniary externalities, it is reasonable to expect trading to reduce the distributional polarization of value vectors, based on the same principle as in the case of an incomplete market. However, nothing points to the possibility of even partial alignment between the value vectors, except by chance. Trading on the market does not mitigate the dimensional polarization of the value vectors. Thus, a positive albeit more ambiguous response can be given to the question raised.

But if there is one question to which analysis of imperfect markets provides a hopeful response, it is the reverse: does democracy lend a helping hand to the market by facilitating the *efficient* allocation of resources?

3.1.2 When Democracy Attenuates Market Failure

A perfect market does more than generate agreement between shareholders: it makes them agree on the most efficient production choice for the economy as a whole. Not only does the market work, but it works in the right direction. This coincidence between what happens and what is desirable is a little miracle. This is the first theorem of the economics of welfare, without doubt the strongest argument in favor of the market.

On an imperfect or incomplete market, the miracle ceases. If shareholders act willy-nilly, how can they ever hope to make an efficient decision? But there is hope, and it is based on the properties of the majority principle. To illustrate this, consider the case of direct production externalities, using the example of firm A which inflicts a negative externality (pollution, for example) on firm B. To keep it simple, suppose A plans to make a decision that will increase the value of its products by one euro but decrease that of B's product by w euros. Leaving moral issues to one side, if $1 - w \geq 0$, the decision is beneficial overall and therefore efficient; if $1 - w < 0$, it is no longer efficient. A shareholder in firm A with no shares in B will favor the decision without any consideration for the harm inflicted on B. Conversely, a shareholder in firm B with no shares in A will oppose the decision without any consideration for the benefit available to A. Here, neither one facilitates the social optimum. By contrast, a shareholder with equal shareholdings in A and B will evaluate the decision by considering precisely its overall impact $1 - w$; this is the only shareholder whose individual incentive is aligned with the social optimum.

Two lessons can be learned from this simple example. The first is that share-holders evaluate decisions relating to production through their portfolios, as specified in Equation (1.4). The second is that only a diversified portfolio with equal shareholdings (a fraction of the market portfolio 1_J) generates the right social incentives: shareholders with such portfolios will favor efficient decisions while all others are biased and will either favor too much externality or not enough.

At this stage a simple but crucial observation can be made; it is that *on average consumers do hold a fraction of the market portfolio*, whether we consider their initial or equilibrium portfolios; this is the result of the market clearing conditions:

$$\sum_i \theta_i = 1_J.$$

Put differently, the *mean consumer* (if one allows this formula in lieu of 'a mean of the consumers') holds a fraction of the market portfolio, and by promoting her individual interests she promotes the social optimum (see Remark 3.1). Put differently again, on average individual interests are in line with the general interest.

A similar observation can be made in the context of imperfect competition. The individual interest of a consumer is aligned with the general interest if this consumer chooses a zero trade, which occurs when the consumer is satisfied with her initial resources (i.e. $x_i^* = \bar{x}_i + Y\bar{\theta}_i$, or $z_i^* = 0_\ell$). Such a consumer does not necessarily exist, but *the market clearing mechanism places the zero trade at the center of gravity of the distribution of trades*, indeed:

$$\sum_i z_i = 0_\ell.$$

Hence, here too, the individual interest of the mean consumer is aligned with the general interest.

The crucial question now relates to the role played by the mean consumer in firm policy. If we agree that good governance should favor the social optimum, then we can also state that *good governance should give power to the mean consumer*.

3.1.3 Shareholder Governance or Stakeholder Democracy?

The mean voter theorem of Caplin & Nalebuff here takes on a significant scope. When interpreted extensively, it predicts that the ideal choice for the mean voter is likely to ultimately prevail as it is stable for (a proxy of) the lowest rate required for a super majority. Imagine a governance system in which *the mean voter and the mean consumer coincide.* Hey presto: the majority vote favors the social optimum. To put it more boldly: democracy is efficient.

But what is this governance system in which the mean voter and the mean consumer are one and the same? On imperfect markets, it is stakeholder democracy, a governance system in which all economic agents, whether or not they hold shares in the firm, can have their say in every decision that affects their welfare. This governance approach differs from the census suffrage of shareholder governance in two ways: everyone votes, not only shareholders; and everyone has just one vote rather than a vote for every share held.

The comparative merits of these two governance systems are reviewed throughout this chapter. Stakeholder democracy appears to be more efficient in the presence of externalities (see Proposition 3.1 and the section that follows) and in the context of imperfect competition (see Proposition 3.2 and the section that follows); as for census suffrage, it is superior in the context of incomplete financial markets (see Corollaries 3.4 and 3.5). Choosing the best governance approach can be tricky unless we again adopt the liberal point of view, which, using reverse logic, asserts that political and economic institutions naturally tend to select efficient governance systems (Rogowski and Linzer 2008a; Rogowski et al., 2008b) and that in the long term, as a result, more census-based systems should emerge in firms suffering from market incompleteness, and more democratic systems in firms facing production externalities or operating in the context of imperfect competition.

Beyond such practical or ideological considerations, what it is hoped this chapter will highlight is the complementarity between the trading and voting mechanisms that can improve total welfare. Structural forces are at work which ensure that each one mitigates the failures of the other.

Section 3.2 reveals the root causes of this complementarity in the presence of external production effects; it highlights the fundamental role played by the diversification of portfolios. Section 3.3 does the same in the context of imperfect competition; it highlights the role played by net trades. Section 3.4 shows how trading on even an incomplete market reduces both the dimensional (Theorem 3.2) and distributional (Proposition 3.4) polarization of the electorate. Propositions 3.1 and 3.2 and Corollary 3.5 in each of the sections lay out the conditions of political stability underlying economically efficient decisions. Section 3.5 shows how the game of expectations can unravel the complementarity between the trading and voting mechanisms and generate inextricable chaos. Lastly, Section 3.6 offers some concluding comments that paves the way to the second part of the book, which explores how collective decisions help shape individual preferences.

3.2 Portfolios

The political economy of firms facing production externalities can be made simple and transparent by looking at the special role played by portfolios. A snapshot of the factors that determine whether or not there is alignment between shareholders and the way in which the majority principle translates into value maximization can be found in the distribution of portfolios. The objective is to shed light on this simple structure. In particular, Corollary 3.1 reflects Proposition 2.3 and shows that making decisions by a majority vote is equivalent to maximizing a weighted sum of firm profits, where the weightings lie within the intersection of the positive cones of the portfolios of all decisive coalitions of voters.

We can use this description to determine the conditions under which decisions reached by vote are efficient. The prominent role played by the market portfolio needs to be emphasized: consumers holding the market portfolio are incentivized to perfectly internalize externalities and promote economic efficiency (Remark 3.1). One central question is: in which governance system is economically efficient production most likely to be politically stable? Proposition 3.1 shows why stakeholder democracy is better positioned to favor efficiency than shareholder governance. This argument hinges on the mean voter theorem: the mean voter is potentially a decision-maker, and in stakeholder democracy he holds the market portfolio.

These arguments are corroborated by the Grassmann approach. The argument presented is that the random nature of externalities transforms the worst scenario in terms of portfolio diversification (where each firm is owned exclusively by a single individual) into an ideal configuration in which simple majority can generate an equilibrium—one that is also efficient (Theorem 3.1).

3.2.1 The Role of Portfolios

Remember that in the presence of production externalities the value vector of consumer i for firm j takes the form given by Equation (1.4)

$$\nabla_{ij}(p, a) = \Xi_j \bar{\theta}_i.$$

Decision a_j is said to be a solution for value vector ∇_{ij} or for (all consumers holding) portfolio $\bar{\theta}_i$ indifferently.

Suppose that, as in Proposition 2.1, a_j is a solution for a value vector in the positive cone of the value vectors of the consumers in $\mathcal{M}$:

$$\nabla_j = \sum_{i \in \mathcal{M}} \mu_{ij} \nabla_{ij} \text{ with } \mu \in \mathbb{R}_{++}^{|\mathcal{M}|},$$

then

$$\nabla_j = \sum_{i \in \mathcal{M}} \mu_{ij} \Xi_j \bar{\theta}_i = \Xi_j \left(\sum_{i \in \mathcal{M}} \mu_{ij} \bar{\theta}_i \right).$$

This means a_j is a solution for a portfolio in the positive cone $\angle^+ \left(\bar{\theta}_i \right)_{i \in \mathcal{M}}$ of the portfolios of the consumers in $\mathcal{M}$. This reveals the special role played by portfolios in regulating production externalities.

Instead of studying the J distributions of individual value vectors $\left(\nabla_{ij} \right)_{i \in \mathcal{I}}$, we can simply study the distribution of portfolios $\left(\bar{\theta}_i \right)_{i \in \mathcal{I}}$. In this way, we analyze the political stability of the decisions in all firms at the same time, as is clear from the following immediate corollary of Proposition 2.3.

Corollary 3.1 *Let* (p^*, x^*, a^*) *be a* ρ–*majority equilibrium. In each firm* j, *decision* a_j^* *maximizes the value of production for a portfolio in the intersection of the positive cones of the portfolios of all decisive coalitions:*

$$\exists \bar{\theta} \in \bigcap_{\mathcal{M} \in \mathcal{D}_j^\rho} \angle^+ \left(\bar{\theta}_i \right)_{i \in \mathcal{M}} \text{ such that } a_j^* = \arg\max \left\{ p^* \cdot Y(a_j, a_{-j}^*) \bar{\theta} \mid a_j \in \mathcal{A}_j \right\}.$$

We will now use this corollary to study the conditions under which externalities are efficiently internalized at equilibrium.

3.2.2 Efficiency

A review of the conditions for the efficient internalization of externalities reveals the prominent role played by the market portfolio: whoever holds this portfolio is incentivized to promote efficient internalization. A ρ–majority equilibrium is efficient if all decisions are solutions for the market portfolio.

One knows that efficient internalization occurs when decisions maximize the joint profit of all firms. Hence the following result.

Lemma 3.1 *Let* (p^*, x^*, y) *be an equilibrium where* $y = f(a)$. *The allocation* (x^*, y) *is optimal if and only if*

$$\text{for every } j, \text{ there is } \beta_j > 0 \text{ such that } \beta_j \nabla_j = \Xi_j 1_J.$$

Hence the following observation.

Remark 3.1 *Efficient internalization in firm* j *occurs if* a_j *is a solution for the market portfolio* 1_J.

This means that efficient internalization occurs in economies in which all investors hold the market portfolio, as is the case in the CAPM model: see Lemma 1.6 and Section 1.3.5. It is noteworthy that as well as the usual benefits associated with safeguarding against risks, portfolio diversification offers additional and fortuitous benefits for consumers by ensuring the efficient internalization of externalities (Hansen & Lott, 1996).

For the (general) scenario in which portfolios are not perfectly diversified, shareholders are biased in the internalization process. Let $\check{\theta}_i = (\sum_j \theta_{ij})/J$ represent the mean number of shares which shareholder i holds in the J firms. During the internalization process, shareholder i will put too much weight on the value of the firms in which he holds a number of shares greater than the mean ($\theta_{ij} > \check{\theta}_i$), and too little weight on the value of the firms in which he holds a number of shares lower than the mean ($\theta_{ij} < \check{\theta}_i$).

Market forces which push for efficient internalization nonetheless remain. By imposing $1_J = \sum_i \bar{\theta}_i$, the market clearing mechanism places the market portfolio 1_J at the center of gravity of the portfolio distribution. In this way, shareholder biases in the internalization process are eliminated on average. On average, shareholders are incentivized to favor efficient internalization. The key question here is: which governance system and which conditions will ensure that this elimination of shareholder bias leads to an efficient decision?

3.2.3 The Political Economy of Efficient Internalization

It is worth mentioning one immediate consequence of the market clearing equation $1_J = \sum_i \bar{\theta}_i$: if there is unanimity between stakeholders in relation to a given decision, then it is an efficient decision. Indeed, given Equation (1.4) one obtains

$$\sum_i \nabla_{ij} = \Xi_j 1_J,$$

and therefore, if there is alignment between all shareholders (all ∇_{ij} are collinear and in the same direction within firm j), then they will unanimously favor an efficient decision.

Furthermore, a corollary of Proposition 2.2 is that the Pareto principle with transfers guarantees efficient decisions.

Corollary 3.2 *Let (p^*, x^*, y) be an equilibrium where $y = f(a)$. Then (x^*, y) is Pareto-optimal if and only if in each firm j the value vector ∇_j respects the Pareto principle with transfers.*

This observation comes as no surprise since we know that allowing transfers amounts to establishing a market on which externalities can be traded, a mechanism which we know restores the efficiency of allocations (provided consumers sincerely reveal their private valuations of goods and services).

What of the majority principle? The following result establishes that efficient internalization is possible at equilibrium if the market portfolio lies in the intersection of the positive cones of the portfolios of decisive coalitions.

Proposition 3.1 *Consider a given economy.*

- *Suppose*

$$1_J \in \bigcap_j \bigcap_{M \in D_j^\rho} \angle^+ \left(\bar{\theta}_i \right)_{i \in M},$$

there are then ρ–majority equilibria with efficient internalization under a system of shareholder governance.
- *Suppose*

$$1_J \in \bigcap_{M \in D^\rho} \angle^+ \left(\bar{\theta}_i \right)_{i \in M},$$

there are then ρ–majority equilibria with efficient internalization under a system of stakeholder democracy.

This proposition allows us to compare the merits of shareholder governance and stakeholder democracy in terms of economic efficiency. In particular, we can see that the conditions for efficient internalization are less strict in the case of stakeholder democracy.

3.2.4 The Case for Stakeholder Democracy

When it comes to the *allocative efficiency* of decisions, stakeholder democracy is liable to perform better than shareholder governance. The key argument is that stakeholder democracy causes the market portfolio to coincide with that of the mean voter. The traditional findings of social choice theory here become operative. In particular, there are efficient ρ–majority equilibria both where $\rho = 0.5$ for symmetrical portfolio distributions, and where $\rho = 0.64$ for portfolios drawn independently from σ-concave distributions (Theorem 2.2).

In contrast, under a system of shareholder governance, the mean voter's portfolio in firm j is $\sum_i \bar{\theta}_{ij} \bar{\theta}_i$ and typically does *not* coincide with the market portfolio. In this case, no evidence has been provided of a class of distributions that would place the market portfolio near the mean or median (multivariate) portfolio.

We will now focus on *productive efficiency*.

Definition 3.1 *Decisions $a \in A$ are productively efficient if and only if there are no other decisions $a' \in A$ such that $f_j^h(a') \geq f_j^h(a)$ for every j and h and $f(a') \neq f(a)$.*

When it comes to productive efficiency, stakeholder democracy is again liable to perform better than shareholder governance. Under the former, decisive coalitions are the same in every firm. So where

$$\bigcap_{M \in \mathcal{D}^{\rho}} \angle^+ (\bar{\theta}_i)_{i \in M} \bigcap \mathbb{R}^J_{++} \neq \emptyset,$$

firms can use the same profit weightings and choose productively efficient plans.

Under a system of shareholder governance, decisive coalitions generally differ from one firm to the next. And if two firms, j and j', are such that the intersection of the positive cones of the portfolios of their decisive coalitions is empty:

$$\bigcap_{M \in \mathcal{D}^{\rho}_j \cup \mathcal{D}^{\rho}_{j'}} \angle^+ (\bar{\theta}_i)_{i \in M} = \emptyset,$$

then they will not use the same profit weightings and their plans will be productively inefficient.

3.2.5 Random Externalities, Efficiency Assured

Proposition 3.1 highlights the worst possible configuration within the portfolio space in terms of internalization. This occurs when the market portfolio is
not contained in the positive cone of the portfolios of any coalition—except of
course that of the grand coalition, i.e. when

$$1_J \in \angle^+ (\theta_i)_{i \in \mathcal{M}} \Rightarrow \mathcal{M} \equiv \mathcal{I}$$

Without loss of generality, we can study this configuration in more detail
by concentrating on an economy made up of as many firms as consumers,
$I = J$ (and $\mathcal{I}$ is identified with $\mathcal{J}$), and in which each consumer is the sole
shareholder in a single firm; this is called a *sole proprietorship economy*. The
portfolio of consumer i is therefore: $\theta_i = (0, \ldots, 0, 1, 0, \ldots, 0)$, whereby the
only non-null component, equal to 1, is in ith position. The portfolios are at
the vertices of a unit simplex (therefore spherico-regular) in $\mathbb{R}^I$. One might
think that such an economy is the worst possible economy from the point of
view of internalizing production externalities, as each consumer maximizes
the profit of her individual firm without any consideration for the external
effects caused. However, under a system of stakeholder democracy, all consumers vote in all companies, and the unpredictability of external effects can,
within the space of the value vectors, paradoxically bring about a configuration
that is much less unfavorable than the one in the portfolio space.

The individual value vectors $(\nabla_{ij})_i$ are the linear transformations via the
operator Ξ_j of the vertices of the portfolio simplex, which naturally points to
reliance on the Grassmann approach from Section 2.5.

Direct production externalities can come in many different forms; in the
model, the ways in which the operator Ξ_j projects the portfolio $\theta_i \in \mathbb{R}^I$ onto
$\mathbb{R}^\ell$ are as numerous as they are varied. From a position of ignorance, it is best
to adopt a Laplacian perspective and assume this projection to be random—
as understood in the Grassmanian approach. Up to an affine transformation,
the I-tuplet of value vectors $(\nabla_{ij})_{i \in \mathcal{J}}$ coincides in distribution with that of
a (standard centered) Gaussian sample in $\mathbb{R}^\ell$. This means that if I is big
compared to ℓ, the worst possible configuration in the portfolio space from the
point of view of internalization (a sole proprietorship economy) is transformed
into the best possible configuration in the space of the vector values, with
(because the Gaussian distribution is symmetrical) the existence of ρ–majority
equilibria for super majority percentages close to 0.5; and (because the sample

is centered) the 0.5^+-majority equilibrium statistically comes with efficient internalization.

Theorem 3.1 *Fix ℓ and consider a stakeholder democracy. When J tends towards infinity, then with probability 1 the min–max score converges towards 0.5, and the min–max set of value vectors $(\nabla_{ij})_{i \in \mathcal{J}}$ is reduced to the efficient value vector.*

3.3 Trades

The political economy of firms operating in the context of imperfect competition can also be made simple and transparent, this time by looking at the special role played by trades. A snapshot of the factors that determine whether or not there is alignment between shareholders and the way in which the majority principle translates into value maximization can be found in the distribution of trades. This section is divided into four parts. The objective is first to elucidate this structure. Then it is necessary to define efficient decisions, and determine the conditions under which decisions taken by vote can be efficient (Proposition 3.2). The prominent role played by the zero trade needs to be emphasized: the no-trade consumers are incentivized to promote economic efficiency. Finally, arguments are provided in favor of stakeholder democracy over shareholder governance when it comes to facilitating economic efficiency.

3.3.1 The Role of Net Trades

Remember that in the case of a monopoly, the value vector of consumer i to value plans in firm j takes the form given by Equation (1.5):

$$\nabla_i(p, x_i, y) = \bar{\theta}_i p - \Phi z_i.$$

The set of plans preferred by a consumer over the status quo is not necessarily convex due to potential price changes, and so the principle of minimal differentiation does not apply. The analysis carried out in this section is local in scope and relates to a limited selection of equilibrium prices.

Assuming y is a solution for a value vector in the positive cone generated by the value vectors of the members of $\mathcal{M}$:

$$\nabla = \sum_{i \in M} \mu_i \nabla_i \text{ where } \mu \in \mathbb{R}_{++}^{|M|},$$

then

$$\nabla = \left(\sum_{i \in M} \mu_i \bar{\theta}_i \right) p - \Phi \left(\sum_{i \in M} \mu_i z_i \right).$$

The model's structure therefore allows us to describe the political stability of efficient allocations based on the distribution of trades.

3.3.2 Efficiency

Optimal allocations are obtained when the value of production is optimized with respect to the market prices.

Lemma 3.2 *Let (p^*, x^*) be an equilibrium for plan y. The allocation (x^*, y) is efficient if and only if there is $\beta > 0$ such that $\beta \nabla = p^*$.*

This is the traditional condition of Pareto optimality: (1) all normalized gradients of consumers' utilities are identical—let us say they are equal to p^*; and (2) plan y maximizes profit with respect to this common price vector: $y = \arg\max\{p^* \cdot y', \ y' \in \mathcal{Y}\}$.

One important observation here is that a no-trade consumer (for whom $z_i = 0$) is incentivized to promote efficient production. In general, all consumers engage in trade and so none of them has the 'right' incentives. There is nonetheless a market logic which can facilitate efficient production. By imposing $\sum_i z_i = 0_\ell$, *the market clearing places the zero trade at the center of gravity of the distribution of trades*. In this way, consumer bias is eliminated on average.

3.3.3 The Political Economy of Efficient Production

Consider an equilibrium (p^*, x^*) for plan y, then market clearing yields, given Equation (1.5),

$$\sum_{i \in \mathcal{I}} \nabla_i = p^*.$$

Therefore, as in the case of direct production externalities, if all consumers are aligned (the ∇_i's are collinear), they will unanimously favor efficient production. This is the case, for example, at no-trade equilibria.

Furthermore, a corollary of Proposition 2.2 is that the Pareto principle with transfers guarantees efficient production.

Corollary 3.3 *Let (p^*, x^*) be an equilibrium for plan y. Then (x^*, y) is efficient if and only if the value vector ∇ respects the Pareto principle with transfers.*

Once again, this observation comes as no surprise since we know that allowing transfers amounts to establishing a market on which the pecuniary externalities resulting from the market power of a monopoly can be traded, a mechanism which we know restores the efficiency of allocations (provided consumers sincerely reveal their private evaluations of goods and services).

What of the majority principle? The following result establishes that efficient production is possible at equilibrium if the zero trade 0_ℓ lies in the intersection of the positive cones of the trades of decisive coalitions.

Proposition 3.2 *Assume*

$$ 0_\ell \in \bigcap_{M \in \mathcal{D}^\rho} \angle^+ (z_i)_{i \in M}, $$

then efficient production is ρ–stable.

This proposition once again allows us to laud the merits of stakeholder democracy when it comes to economic efficiency.

3.3.4 The Case for Stakeholder Democracy

In the context of imperfect competition, as in the case of direct production externalities, stakeholder democracy is liable to perform better than shareholder governance in terms of the *allocative* efficiency of decisions. The key argument is that *stakeholder democracy causes the zero trade to coincide with that of the mean voter.* The traditional findings of social choice theory can once again be used here. In particular, there are efficient ρ–majority equilibria both where $\rho = 0.5$ for symmetrical distributions of net trades, and where $\rho = 0.64$ when the distribution of net trades is σ-concave (Theorem 2.2).

In contrast, under a system of shareholder governance, the mean voter's trade is $\sum_i \bar{\theta}_i z_i$ and typically does *not* coincide with the zero trade. In this case, no evidence has been provided of a class of distributions that would place the zero trade near the mean or median (multivariate) trade.

3.4 Present Values

Incomplete markets allow us to analyze the interaction between the trading and voting mechanisms in the most detail. Specifically, they enable us to understand how *trading on the market reduces the conflict dimensions in the electorate*, thereby facilitating the democratic process (Theorem 3.2). The textbook scenario presented in Section 1.2 is used to illustrate Theorem 3.2 where it overlaps with the median voter theorem, and to show in a simple framework how the principle of minimal differentiation operates and where a stable production plan is positioned.

Following a brief review of an adapted concept of efficiency (Definition 3.2), the most efficient possible production plans are identified (Corollary 3.4), and conditions that would ensure their political stability with super majority rates close to the stability threshold are proposed (Corollary 3.5 and Proposition 3.4). We show how *trading on the market reduces the distributional polarization of electorates.*

3.4.1 When Trading Attenuates the Polarization in Dimension

One of the messages in this essay is that the lowest super majority threshold ρ for which there is at least one politically stable market equilibrium (the economy's stability threshold) measures the extent of the democratic failure. The democratic failure refers to the difficulty the voting mechanism has in producing collective choices that are politically stable without having to impose an excessively high super majority.

As emphasized in the previous chapter, the configuration for the division of a cake is the worst possible configuration from this point of view, because either nothing is stable or every consumer has veto power and everything is stable. Close to the opposite end of the spectrum, one finds the case of one-dimensional single-peaked preferences for which there are stable choices for the simple majority, which by definition does not give veto power to any minority. The question here is: where does the scenario of an incomplete market lie on the spectrum of this dilemma?

We saw in Section 1.3 that the market contributes to the resolution of conflict between shareholders by reducing the number of conflict dimensions. In the absence of trading, there are potential conflicts according to the ℓ dimensions of the space of value vectors. When J assets are traded (with $J \le \ell$) disagreements are completely eliminated along the J dimensions of the space of financial transactions, and can only remain along the $\ell - J$ dimensions of the complementary sub-space. Using Greenberg's approach, we can see that trading improves the stability threshold of the economy.

Theorem 3.2 *(Tvede & Crès, 2005) There is a ρ-majority equilibrium if and only if*

$$\rho \ge \frac{\ell - J}{\ell - J + 1}.$$

Of course, when the number of missing assets is high, the political gain (in terms of improving the stability threshold) generated by creating additional assets to complete the financial structure is low. The important message in Theorem 3.2 is that the interaction between trading and voting works in the right direction and favors the political stability of economic equilibria.

The scenario of an almost complete market ($J = \ell - 1$) merits particular attention because here equilibrium is achieved for the simple majority.

3.4.2 The Median Voter and Minimal Differentiation

To show how the median voter theorem works in this framework, we will return to the textbook scenario of linear quadratic utility functions (with consumption at date 0) with, for the purposes of clarityity, only two states of the world and one firm: $\ell = 2$ and $J = 1$.

To simplify as much as possible, consider two equiprobable states of the world $\pi^1 = \pi^2 = 0.5$ (the π-distance is therefore the Euclidean distance). Let us further assume that consumers have the same risk tolerance coefficient ($\gamma_i = \Gamma/I$) and differ only in terms of their endowments, which are distributed along the segment from $B = (1/\sqrt{I}, -1/\sqrt{I})$ to $C = (-1/\sqrt{I}, 1/\sqrt{I})$, such that there is no aggregate risk: $\sum_i \bar{x}_i = 0$. Finally, we will assume that the set of production plans $\mathcal{Y} \subset \mathbb{R}^2$ is defined as

$$\mathcal{Y} = \{y \in \mathbb{R}_+^2 \mid \|y\| \le \sqrt{I}\}.$$

At equilibrium (q^*, x^*, θ^*, y), immediate calculations based on the proof of Lemma 1.6 give us a simple expression for the optimal portfolio and bundle of consumer i:

$$\theta_i^* = \frac{1}{I}(1 - \bar{x}_i \cdot y) \text{ and } x_i^* = \bar{x}_i + \frac{1}{I}(1 - \bar{x}_i \cdot y)\,y.$$

We can see in Fig. 3.1[2] that x^* is the orthogonal projection of $\bar{x}$ onto the straight line tangent to $\mathcal{Y}$ at y, denoted as T_y.

Given that utility is decreasing with the Euclidean distance from consumption $\bar{x} + \theta y$ to ideal consumption $\gamma 1_\ell$, when a consumer faces the choice between the status quo y and an alternative y' she will favor the alternative over the status quo if $\|\gamma 1_\ell - \bar{x} - \theta y\| > \|\gamma 1_\ell - \bar{x} - \theta y'\|$; therefore, if the consumer's portfolio is positive, she will favor the alternative over the status quo if and only if

$$\gamma 1_\ell \cdot (y' - y) > \bar{x} \cdot (y' - y).$$

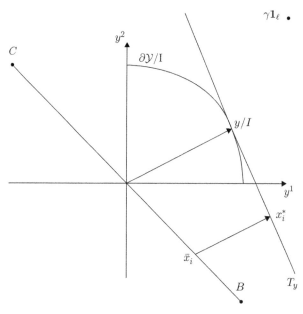

Fig. 3.1 Optimal consumption x^*

---

[2] The production plans y are normalized for the purposes of simplifying the notation and the drawings. In the figures, it is the normalized production set $\mathcal{Y}/I$ that is represented.

Let us define the line Δ of equation $(\gamma 1_\ell - \bar{x}) \cdot (y' - y) = 0$ (for which the above inequality is an equality: see Fig. 3.2). It cuts the segment $[B, C]$ at $\bar{x}_\Delta$, which is an endowment for which the consumer is indifferent between the status quo y and the alternative y', insofar as for all $\theta > 0$, $\bar{x}_\Delta + \theta y$ and $\bar{x}_\Delta + \theta y'$ lie at the same distance from the ideal bundle $\gamma 1_\ell$ (Δ bisects the angle between these two vectors).

The analysis can therefore be carried out using a Hotelling-type model (1929) in Fig. 3.2. Consumers whose endowments $\bar{x}$ are below Δ will prefer the alternative y', and those whose endowments $\bar{x}$ are above Δ will prefer the status quo y.

As the alternative y' shifts towards the status quo y, the line Δ pivots clockwise around $\gamma 1_\ell$. The dotted line in Fig. 3.2 shows the limit position Δ^{lim} of Δ when y' tends towards y. We can see that the alternative y' receives more support as it shifts towards the status quo y, and by getting as close as possible to it (minimal differentiation principle): here, all consumers whose endowments are in the segment $[B, \bar{x}_\Delta^{\text{lim}}]$ support the alternative y'. At the limit, the consumers who keep supporting the status quo are those whose endowments are in the segment $[C, \bar{x}_\Delta^{\text{lim}}]$.

It follows from the minimal differentiation principle that the best strategy y^* for the status quo is to place itself from the outset at the median of the

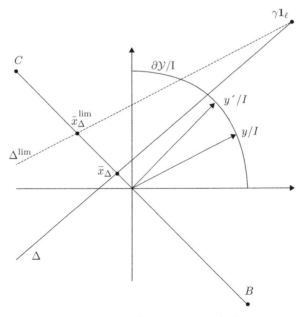

Fig. 3.2 The challenger y' competing with the status quo y

distribution of the electoral weights;[3] it is then stable for the simple majority. If the endowments are symmetrically distributed around 0, then y^* is the vector at 45°.

So much for the equilibrium. We will now turn to the normative analysis of what happens on the markets and at GAs and talk about efficiency.

3.4.3 Constrained Efficiency

When studying the efficiency of the market, one underlying question is: could a central planner do better than the market by reallocating goods herself? When the market is incomplete, this is not difficult: it is simply a question of reallocating goods across *all* states of the world—which the market would allow if it were complete.

This raises a more pertinent question: could a central planner do better than the market if she faced the same constraints? This brings us to the concept of *constrained efficiency*. Let us assume that the planner cannot reallocate goods directly but only through portfolios and by changing the asset structure.

An allocation (x, y) is said to be *constrained-feasible* if $x_i - \bar{x}_i \in \langle Y \rangle$ for every i. Let $\mathcal{F}(\bar{x})$ be the set of constrained-feasible allocations:

$$\mathcal{F}(\bar{x}) = \left\{ (x, y) \in \mathbb{R}^{\ell I} \times \Pi_j \mathcal{Y}_j \mid \forall i, \ x_i - \bar{x}_i \in \langle Y \rangle \right\}.$$

Definition 3.2 *An allocation (x, y) is constrained-efficient if (i) $(x, y) \in \mathcal{F}(\bar{x})$ and (ii) there is no other allocation $(x', y') \in \mathcal{F}(\bar{x})$ such that $u_i(x_i') \geq u_i(x_i)$ for every i with at least one strict inequality.*

One of the difficulties is that $\mathcal{F}(\bar{x})$ is not convex. This is due to the interplay between the choice of portfolio θ_i and the choice of plans y to define $x_i = \bar{x}_i + Y\theta_i$; the term $Y\theta_i$ is quadratic and therefore non-concave. This adds a limitation to the analysis because the necessary first-order conditions for the planner's constrained optimization program are not sufficient. They will have to do.

3.4.4 The Political Economy of Constrained Efficiency

Consider stability in light of the Pareto principle with transfers. At equilibrium $(q^*, x^*, \theta^*, y^*)$, sustainable transfers $(w_i)_{i \in I_j}$ associated with a change in production Δy for firm j modify the consumption of consumer i from x_i^*

---

[3] To apply the median voter theorem, either the set of endowments or the production set must be unidimensional; here, both sets are unidimensional for the purposes of simplicity.

to $x_i^* + \theta_{ij}^* \Delta y + w_i 1_\ell$. According to Lemma 1.3, the consumer will support this change if

$$\nabla_i^{\parallel}(x_i^*) \cdot (\theta_{ij}^* \Delta y + w_i 1_\ell) > 0 \Longleftrightarrow \nabla_i(x_i^*) \cdot \Delta y + w_i > 0,$$

where $\nabla_i(x_i^*) = \theta_{ij}^* \nabla_i^{\parallel}(x_i^*)$.

A direct corollary of Proposition 2.2 allows us to deduce that equilibrium production plans maximize profits for the *mean value vector* of shareholders, where the mean is weighted according to the number of shares held in the firm.

Corollary 3.4 (*Drèze, 1974*) *An equilibrium* $(q^*, x^*, \theta^*, y^*)$ *is stable in respect of the Pareto principle with transfers if and only if for every j,*

$$y_j^* = \arg\max \left\{ \nabla_j^* \cdot y_j \mid y_i \in \mathcal{Y}_j \right\} \text{ where } \nabla_j^* = \sum_{i \in \mathcal{I}_j} \theta_{ij}^* \nabla_i^{\parallel}(x_i^*).$$

It is therefore a notion of general equilibrium in the strict sense of Definition 1.5.

With such equilibria, the first-order conditions needed for constrained efficiency are satisfied.

Proposition 3.3 *Stable equilibria with respect to the Pareto principle with transfers satisfy the first-order conditions of constrained efficiency. Such equilibria are said to be quasi-optimal.*

One of the central questions in this chapter is now apparent: under which governance system and under which conditions can one hope that the production plans retained at the end of the voting procedure will be quasi-optimal? This would mean that democracy is capable of re-establishing what the market was unable to promote.

3.4.5 When Voting Is (Quasi) Efficient

This section takes a slight liberty with the terminology: in the spirit of Proposition 2.7, a list $(\nabla_i)_{i \in \mathcal{I}}$ of value vectors is said to have a compact and convex support when it can be understood to have originated in independent drawings from a compact and convex support. Similarly, a list of voting weights $(\lambda_{ij})_{i \in \mathcal{I}}$ will be said to be σ-concave when it can be understood to have originated in independent drawings from a distribution with σ-concave density.

An immediate corollary of Theorem 2.2 can be used to describe the stability of quasi-optimal equilibria.

Corollary 3.5 *Consider a quasi-optimal equilibrium; if in each firm the distribution of the value vectors has a compact and convex support and is σ-concave for some $\sigma > 0$, then the considered equilibrium is 0.64–stable.*

3.4.6 When Trading Attenuates the Polarization in Distribution

We must now determine whether the conditions for the validity of this corollary (and in particular the σ-concavity of the value vectors' distribution) can be obtained endogenously through market transactions. The beginning of this chapter emphasized the fact that trading on the market brings together consumers with similar savings and investment needs. Just as Section 3.4.1 shows how the market can reduce the dimensional polarization of an electorate, we will now see why it is reasonable to hope that the value vectors of a single group of shareholders will display *less distributional polarization* than the economy as a whole.

If we try to link the conditions for the validity of Corollary 3.5 to the hypotheses on the model's fundamentals, we must naturally consider (1) a compact and convex set of fundamental consumer characteristics, and (2) linear gradients in relation to these fundamental characteristics and the choice variables. One obvious class is that of quadratic utility functions, in particular the one from our textbook scenario, with parameters: $\iota = (\gamma, \bar{x})$.

Four remarkable properties of this scenario allow us to apply Theorem 2.2: (*i*) as the proof of Lemma 1.6 shows, equilibrium portfolios are linear functions of $\bar{x}$ and do not depend on the initial distribution of the portfolios $\bar{\theta}$; (*ii*) the subset of fundamental characteristics for which the shares held in firm j are positive is convex; (*iii*) in this subset, the electoral weights θ_j^+ linearly depend on the fundamental characteristics; and (*iv*) the gradients $DU(x)$ linearly depend on $\bar{x}$.

Property (*iii*) is of particular interest. The linearity of the equilibrium portfolios is obtained endogenously, illustrating how trading on the market reduces the distributional polarization of the electorate. In order for the 'smoothing' of the distribution to bear fruit, the firm's decisions must be based on the equilibrium portfolios (governance à la Drèze, 1974) rather than the initial portfolios (governance à la Grossman & Hart, 1979). Schematically speaking, the vote must take place after the market has been closed and all transactions have been completed.

The following proposition establishes that if the consumers' initial endowments and portfolios are subjected to a σ-concave shock, a vote with a super majority of 0.64 maintains the political stability of the quasi-optimal equilibria.

Proposition 3.4 *Consider the utility functions (1.2). Assuming that the distribution of the fundamental characteristics has a compact and convex support and is σ-concave, then where $\lambda \equiv \theta^+$ a market equilibrium is 0.64−stable.*[4]

In conclusion, it would appear that shareholder governance based on equilibrium portfolios best enables the virtues of trading to be exploited in terms of reducing conflicts between shareholders and the polarization of the electorate. But it also opens the Pandora's box of expectations, which become a crucial element in what is now not just an economic analysis but also political.

3.5 Expectations

It is well established that expectations can have a destabilizing impact on the economy. All kinds of wild prophecies can become reality simply by being proffered and by attracting a sufficient number of adherents (see footnote 2 in Chapter 4). Through the interaction between the trading and voting mechanisms, the market can contaminate democracy and aggravate its tendency towards chaos by infecting it with the virus of self-fulfilling expectations.

3.5.1 Exit and Stability

At a majority stable equilibrium, shareholders are assumed to have conservative expectations insofar as they expect the current production plan to remain in force. They do not therefore expect that any alternative will replace the status quo. And at equilibrium, these expectations prove well founded: the status quo is unassailable. But what if shareholders deviate from these conservative expectations and forecast the success of a competing plan?

---

[4] In order for the result to be valid under a governance system based on the initial portfolios, further conditions are needed for their distribution: for every j, the distribution of $\bar{\theta}_j^+$ must also have a compact and convex support, and be σ-concave. It is of course possible to reconcile these two perspectives using a dynamic model in which the current initial portfolios are the previous equilibrium portfolios.

If we observe this situation, we can see that everything begins with an equilibrium (q^*, x^*, θ^*) for production plans y^*. Suppose the shareholders expect that the alternative y_j will replace the status quo y_j^* in firm j—we then refer to *exit expectations*. They then expect new prices q and on this basis acquire new optimal portfolios θ, with the result that their transactions are based on their expectation of a new equilibrium (q, x, θ) for the amended production plan $(y_{-j}^*, y_j) = (y_1^*, \ldots, y_{j-1}^*, y_j, y_{j+1}^*, \ldots, y_J^*)$. The outcome of this is that under the status quo y^*, with portfolio θ consumer i consumes bundle $\bar{x}_i + Y^*\theta_i$, which he evaluates based on the value vector $\nabla_i(\bar{x}_i + Y^*\theta_i)$.

What changes in the composition of the group of shareholders do the new portfolios θ bring about? The new plan y_j offers different insurance opportunities from those offered by y_j^*. So shareholders whose needs are less well covered by y_j than by y_j^* will at least partially reduce their stake in the firm. They will be replaced by shareholders whose needs are better covered by y_j than by y_j^*. This increases the electoral weights of those who prefer the alternative, and reduces the electoral weights of those who prefer the status quo, which in turn makes it more likely for the alternative to be adopted. It is clear therefore that exit expectations can only serve to amplify the recomposition of the group of shareholders in a way that validates those expectations.

With such expectations in play, the production plan in place is only stable if it *remains unbeatable even in the electorate newly recomposed by the portfolios* θ and the vector values $\nabla_i(\bar{x}_i + Y^*\theta_i)$. This points to the notion of a stronger stability than ρ–stability (Crès & Tvede, 2009).

Definition 3.3 *A ρ-majority equilibrium (q^*, x^*, y^*) is **exit-stable** if for every j and all alternative plans y_j, given equilibrium (q, x, θ) for the plans (y_{-j}^*, y_j), the firms' value vectors $(\nabla_j^*)_{j\in\mathcal{J}}$ supporting the status quo y^* remain ρ-stable for the portfolios θ and the consumers' value vectors $(\nabla_i(\bar{x}_i + Y^*\theta_i))_{i\in\mathcal{I}}$.*

The use of the term 'exit' is a tribute to the work of Hirschman (1970), who analyzed the attitudes of consumers facing a decline in the quality of a product and distinguished between (*i*) consumers who exit and (*ii*) those who remain loyal but 'voice'.

3.5.2 A Geometric Illustration of the Exit Effect

We will now return to the textbook scenario of Section 3.4, beginning with the median production plan y^* for symmetrically distributed endowments. We know it is 0.5–stable when expectations are conservative and equilibrium shares are identical: $\theta_i^* = 1/I$ for every i.

Next we test its stability under exit expectations. The significant change is that the electoral weights are no longer the (identical) equilibrium shares θ^*, but rather the newly recalculated shares θ, as if all shareholders were anticipating the replacement of the status quo y^* by alternative y.

The political support for the alternative is the result of two opposing effects:

(*i*) First, a standard differentiation effect: if y shifts clockwise away from y^*, the separating line Δ pivots clockwise around $\gamma \mathbf{1}_\ell$, thereby reducing support for alternative y: from $[C, 0]$ to $[C, \bar{x}_\Delta]$ in Fig. 3.3. This differentiation effect produces a *centripetal force* encouraging the alternative to move closer to the status quo.

(*ii*) Second, an exit effect comparable to the price effect in Hotelling's model, linked to the recomposition of the electorate and their electoral weights after the shift in the optimal portfolios from θ^* to θ. It should be remembered that a consumer's stake in the firm is measured by the distance from his endowment (in $[C, B]$) to the tangent T_y. We can see that as y shifts clockwise away from y^*, the quantity of shares held by supporters of y, i.e. those shareholders whose endowments are in $[C, \bar{x}_\Delta]$, increases in relative terms since T_y moves away from $[C, \bar{x}_\Delta]$. At the same time, the quantity of shares held by supporters of y^*, i.e.

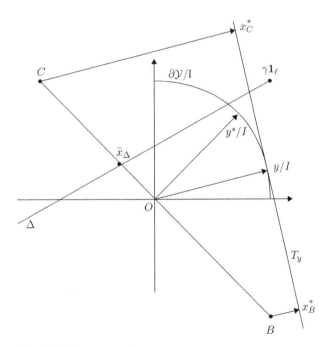

Fig. 3.3 Exit expectations

those shareholders whose endowments are in $[\bar{x}_\Delta, B]$, decreases in relative terms since T_y moves closer to $[\bar{x}_\Delta, B]$. This exit effect produces a *centrifugal force* encouraging the alternative to move away from the status quo.

Which of these two effects dominates? That depends on the model's parameters, of course. We will now look at two examples that reveal possible—and troubling—configurations.

3.5.3 Maximal Differentiation and Deterrence from Exit

One consequence of possible exit expectations is that the stability threshold for exit is higher than that of conservative expectations. Here is an example.

Consider $\gamma_i = 1$ for every i and three consumers ($I = 3$) with endowments in C, O and B. We set the parameters of alternative y using its angle ψ with the abscissa axis: $y = (\cos \psi, \sin \psi)$. The equilibrium shares associated with exit expectations are

$$\theta_C = \frac{1}{3}(1 + \cos \psi - \sin \psi) \qquad \theta_0 = \frac{1}{3} \qquad \theta_B = \frac{1}{3}(1 - \cos \psi + \sin \psi).$$

Clearly, when $0° < \psi < 45°$, consumer C supports the alternative and consumers O and B support the status quo. But the relative electoral weight of consumer C in the voting procedure increases towards 2/3 when ψ tends towards 0. Here, maximal differentiation ($\psi \to 0$) is optimal. It follows that the only way to deter exit expectations is to adopt a super majority of 2/3. In short, to make the 0.5—equilibrium (with conservative expectations) exit-stable, it is necessary to increase the super majority from 1/2 to 2/3.

This leaves us with a paradox. For if $\rho \geq 2/3$, then exit expectations cannot be self-fulfilling, and only conservative expectations are viable at equilibrium. With such expectations, an alternative can at best receive the support of 1/3 of the electorate against the status quo. A super majority of 2/3 is therefore needed to ensure that no alternative will ever generate the support of more than 1/3 of the electorate against the status quo; a super majority that is 'twice too big' is therefore needed. This amounts to using a sledgehammer to crack a nut.[5]

---

[5] Of course, the extent to which the super majority must be raised to deter exit-expectations depends on the distribution of the endowments. In the example above, only the exit effect plays a role: there is no differentiation effect since the position of $\bar{x}_\Delta$ between C and O is of no importance. Things would

3.5.4 When Things Go Awry

Another consequence of possible exit expectations is that the level of chaos in the political process can reach a height never encountered in the standard context of social choice. This is because, *even where a unanimous vote is required ($\rho = 1^-$), there can be Condorcet cycles of length two.*

Consider just two consumers ($I = 2$): one type C and one type B. Consider y_B the plan corresponding to $\psi = 90°$ and y_C the plan corresponding to $\psi = 0°$. Assuming y_B^* is the status quo, at equilibrium $\theta_C^* = 0$ and $\theta_B^* = 1$. Any alternative y where $0° \le \psi < 90°$ will be preferred by C to y_B^*. If both consumers expect that y_C will prevail in the future, then at the new equilibrium: $\theta_C = 1$ and $\theta_B = 0$; consumer B completely relinquishes his stake in the firm and is replaced by consumer C. With this new electorate, y_C receives all of the votes against y_B. Hence, if y_B is the status quo then y_C beats y_B unanimously. The symmetrical line of reasoning shows that the reverse is also true: if y_C is the status quo then y_B beats y_C unanimously. Hence a cycle of length two that no super majority rate can eliminate. It is difficult to imagine a more chaotic social choice configuration.

3.6 Preferences

It should be clear by now that the study of collective choices is arduous. Endeavors to structure problems in a clear manner are often shattered by the eruption of a demonic configuration, as in the cases of circular preferences or the division of a cake. This is why the vast majority of the meaningful results of social choice theory point to the impossibility of a rational collective choice. Only collective choices that involve one single conflict dimension escape this curse. And so economists use and abuse unidimensional models to invoke the median voter theorem, because they do not know how else to proceed. This is a somewhat desperate tactic given the many different possible forms of leverage at the disposal of companies. It is also a trap. Although it guarantees an equilibrium for the simple majority, it does so through the artifice of unidimensionality. And above all, this equilibrium is in general not efficient: it is the mean and not the median voter who pushes for efficiency, and the two do not necessarily coincide. This is where the trap shuts: economists use the

---

be different if for example the endowments were uniformly distributed along $[C, B]$. In that case, it would be necessary to raise the super majority from 0.5 to 0.53 to safeguard against exit-expectations.

median voter theorem purely in the interest of technical convenience, but at the cost of skewing their normative analysis of the market.

The political economy of firms laid out in this essay retains the wealth of multidimensional analysis. However, it is based on a resolutely optimistic view in relation to the possibility of a rational collective choice. For the issue being considered, that of *collective choices on the market*, it is possible to remove a certain number of obstacles: a static electorate, equal voting weights, and an immutable ranking of public choices by each voter. In this text, these variables are *endogenous*. Social choice is considered *in general equilibrium*, raising the hope of reconciling economic theory with reality, in particular that of votes at GAs.

Unfortunately it is clear that, however desperate or heroic, these attempts at reconciliation fall far short of the mark. Pessimists will interpret the modest scope of the results presented in this chapter as a clear indication that a mindset of individual optimization is at best orthogonal—and at worst opposed—to the mindsets that orient collective action, and that no social harmony can ever emerge from a cacophony of egos. Optimists will see these results as a basis for believing in the symbiosis between individual choices and collective decisions in our economies, a symbiosis idealized herein by the combined and simultaneous trading and voting mechanisms, which form a lasting and mutually beneficial association. But even the most optimistic of readers will be forced to admit that we are still some way short of explaining the Soviet-era scores with which motions are carried at the GAs of firms on the CAC 40.

The only economist whose faith remains unshaken is the hard-core liberal, for whom such attempts to reconcile economic theory with the reality of voting at GAs are neither desperate nor heroic, but quite simply futile. He would have preferred to see this essay come to a close at the end of the second paragraph in the introduction, for the overwhelming scores clearly provide further proof of the market's perfection; the 6 or 14 percent by which the mean scores fall short of the theoretical prediction of unanimity are at worst slip-ups, and at best the exception that proves the rule.

This attitude of contempt is shared by the economist who denies that economic theory has any capacity to explain social phenomena. He will reject our attempts at reconciliation as absurd, arguing that the rational individual is a figment of the imagination, that shareholder democracy is a fool's gold, and that the perfect market is a deadly ideology. He sees the staggering ease with which motions are carried at CAC 40 GAs as the result of opaque dealings between powerful parties (top executives and senior civil servants) and of the economic and intellectual dictatorship through which they reign over small shareholders. Seen from this perspective, the 6 or 14 precent margins shy of absolute unanimity are a measure of resistance against oppression.

Caught between the two, our tempered neoclassical economist is desperate to rebel. He wants emancipation from the rigorous vision of the first, and is intent on countering the nihilistic vision of the second. To do this, his neoclassical foundations must remain steadfast, but another obstacle must be removed: that of methodological individualism in its most extreme form, where no social influence can modify individual preferences. The first part of this essay scrupulously complied with this methodology: the utility functions $(U_i)_{i \in \mathcal{I}}$ are determined from the outside and set in stone. Part II adopts a more holistic method and considers how collective decisions in turn have an impact on the formation of these preferences.

PART II

THE SOCIAL ECONOMY OF THE SHAREHOLDER

Part I of this essay described the political economy of the firm, eschewing the rational choice paradigm as well as any notion of limited rationality: firms are not endowed with reason and therefore have no will or objective function. All they have are management bodies and a governance structure, and what we see when we look at firms is that decisions are taken following board meetings and GAs. Politically stable decisions were identified, the only ones that can establish regularity. This regularity is the result of the interplay of forces at work within the firm, in application of the procedures set out in the governance system and in accordance with a protocol which can at times seem mechanical. The objective of Part I was to model the mechanism through which these forces are combined, in an effort to explore the black box of firms in a context of general equilibrium.

Homo monolithicus

But the analysis continued to see the individuals themselves as rational agents in the strictest sense of the term. They remained within the confines of mono-lithic rationality, represented by a measurable objective function—utility. This was both useful and fruitful as an initial approach, but one senses the need for a more flexible approach to individual rationality. For agents play many different roles. As consumers, they exchange goods and services; as investors, they adjust their asset portfolios to their savings and insurance needs; as share-holders, they express their opinions in various forums and try to influence the decision-making process within the firm. In each of these roles, they are exposed to the dynamics of the individuals and collective entities around them, beginning with their households, the experts whose skills they draw on, and the shareholders meetings in which they participate.[1] It is difficult to believe that the individual decision-making process itself is so monolithic, just as it is difficult to believe that individual preferences are not themselves the product of a form of aggregation.[2]

The challenge is now to model the mechanism through which these forces are combined internally by the individual, and to open up the black box of preferences in the neoclassical model.

Nothing new so far. Economists have long sought to model individual decisions based on the aggregation of expert judgments.[3] Their models are particularly inspiring for anyone trying to understand investment decisions when faced with an uncertain future. While economic forecasting makes it possible to imagine plausible future scenarios, it is impossible to attribute an objective likelihood of occurrence to each one. At best, an expert will develop an argument that will lead to a plausible value for this likelihood, but such a judgment will always be imbued with subjectivity. It then falls to the decision-maker to exploit the many subjective judgments to which she is exposed and ultimately make a call.

Collective Opinion: Objective Judgment?

This is the most useful vision of individual decision-making when it comes to understanding investment decisions taken by an individual agent, and subsequently determining the collective entities she joins, the opinions she expresses within those entities, and ultimately the proposals she supports. The opinions and judgments on which she draws to form her own opinion are gleaned here and there: in the media, by chance in conversation with other investors and bankers, but also at the shareholders' meetings she attends.

In particular, the proposals made by the board of directors must weigh on the mental process of this shareholder, especially when they are adopted by massive majorities at the GA. For, to some extent, they take on the aspect of a court judgment and necessarily carry the same authority. An individual

---

[1] More generally, located at the intersection between networks of social connections, the individual is subjected to multiple influences and acts in various capacities. This reality has inspired a prolific literature on social—or interdependent—preferences (see Benhabib et al., 2011).

[2] The principle according to which individual preferences expressed on the markets are formed through a process of aggregation is natural enough when one considers the household—rather than the individuals it comprises—to be the decision-making unit (see, for example, Chiappori & Ekeland, 2006, and the literature review included therein). This is also the principle that underpins theory of choice rationalization (see the literature review by Ambrus & Rozen, 2008).

[3] Cf. Crès et al. (2011) and the literature review therein.

opinion is the fruit of one's reflection, inevitably affected by personal experience, one's perceptions and even one's desires and emotions; it may reflect moral considerations or simply one's humor; sometimes it oscillates and randomly settles because the time has come to make a call. In contrast, intuition tells us that an opinion expressed by a collective entity does not suffer from the same biases. Here, contingencies and shifting humors should compensate for one another; desires and emotions should neutralize one another; the multiplicity of individual experiences enriches the decision-making process more than it skews it; and there is nothing to suggest that a group of shareholders at a GA is bereft of authentically diverse moral stances.[4]

Once again, the image that comes to mind is that of a decision reached by a jury. Each juror must develop her own intimate conviction—often irretrievably marked by subjectivity. Their deliberation and their vote combine their individual opinions into a collective judgment, in accordance with an inexorable protocol. Residue from their personal convictions remains, but the gamble inherent in the jury system is that most of the biases they cause will neutralize and compensate for one another, like a statistical hazard: on average. The collective judgment is more objective, not because it is based on observable and opposable facts, but because it is less skewed by personal bias.[5]

In this respect, board decisions adopted at GAs have a tinge of *res judicata*. They are instilled with a kind of wisdom. What is more, they are the product of aggregate expert judgments. By inherently speculating about the future, they are indicative of judgments about the likelihood of possible future scenarios, and this information feeds the reflection of each individual. One could propose a model in which the media, opinion leaders, boards of directors or individual board members—in short, a whole array of agents of influence—intervene between investors and shareholder groups and play a role as intermediaries on the 'market of opinions.' This would provide a more realistic representation of what appears to be a self-referential world, in which individual opinions combine to form collective judgments which in turn feed into individual reflections. But such a model would carry the disadvantage of excessively complicating the analysis without ever really enriching it; and the main message would be the same. The short channels of influence—from GAs to investors, from investors to shareholders, and from shareholders to GAs—constitute a simplification of reality that accounts for the essential. In the art of modelling,

---

[4] Proposition 2.1 suggests that when collectives aggregate individual opinions through a mechanism that respects the Pareto principle, individual biases are eliminated on average.

[5] A more accurate—albeit cumbersome—term is *intersubjectivity* rather than sheer objectivity.

too, it is best to leave well enough alone. In an effort to get closer to reality, one often distorts rather than describes it.

Investment and *Affectio Societatis*

There is another reason why the proposals made by the board of directors weigh on the individual shareholder's decision-making process. It relates to what French law refers to as *affectio societatis*,[6] a common will to invest and share in the same exploit, and thereby share the profits or losses of a firm. The *affectio societatis* at the CAC 40 GAs is of course weaker than within a group of partners in a joint venture, but it serves to filter the first commonalities, those formed by the chance circumstances of one's birth.

Affectio societatis is the result of the self-selection mechanism that brings shareholders together, described in detail and discussed in Chapter 3. Individuals join a group of shareholders by choice, not by force or by chance. They do so because they share certain views about the future as well as certain needs when it comes to consumption and savings. Such a community of views and needs will display more empathy towards the opinions and beliefs of its members, who will feel better understood and protected. Furthermore, the freedom to associate with a particular group has an aspect of meta-choice: one chooses to choose. This is a bit like joining a political party: even though the 'party line' may not totally reflect your personal convictions, you respect it and even adhere to it, or at any rate you do not oppose it as openly as when your affiliation is mandatory.

There is every reason to believe that the strength of this meta-choice, combined with that of the community of views and needs, favors, if not blind adhesion to the opinions of the groups we join of our own accord, then at least a certain benevolence towards them.[7] One of the virtues of *affectio societatis* is that when the collective opinion makes its way to the individual's inner thoughts for reflection, it finds itself on friendly soil.

---

[6] A notion that could be bridged to the 'loyalty' of Hirschman (1970).

[7] In the citation below, Simmel (1955) uses the term 'surrenders,' even though there is no notion of constraint: "As the person becomes affiliated with a social group, he surrenders himself to it." A bit like giving up one's arms in a friendly or romantic exchange.

The Individual–Collective Duality

We will now continue this analysis by looking at the duality between the individual and the collective. Individuals shape the groups they join and at the same time are shaped by them. The notion of duality between individuals and groups has a long-established tradition in sociology. It can be traced back to the late-nineteenth-century work of sociologist Georg Simmel, who argued that the interpenetration between the individual and the groups to which he belongs is central to our understanding of society. The following citation is in this regard particularly revealing:

> [. . .] as individuals, we form the personality out of particular elements of life, each of which has arisen from, or is interwoven with, society. This personality is subjectivity par excellence in the sense that it combines the elements of culture in an individual manner. There is here a reciprocal relation between the subjective and the objective. As the person becomes affiliated with a social group, he surrenders himself to it. A synthesis of such subjective affiliations creates a group in an objective sense. But the person also regains his individuality because his pattern of participation is unique: hence the fact of multiple group-participation creates in turn a new subjective element. Causal determination of, and purposive action by, the individual appear as two sides of the same coin.   (Simmel, 1955, p. 141)

This of course is an affront to the sacrosanct paradigm of methodological individualism,[8] but to some extent we will see that it is broadly compatible with the dominant economic thinking.

When applied to the topic of this essay, the duality hypothesis specifically asserts that collective opinions emerge through the aggregation of individual opinions; and reciprocally, individual opinions are amended through the aggregation of collective opinions. What does this reciprocal aggregation bring about? This is what we will explore in the next chapter.

[8] Although List & Spiekermann (2013) assert that 'supervenience individualism' (the view that individual-level facts fully determine social facts) is compatible with 'causal-explanatory holism' (the view that some causal relations are distinct from any individual-level causal relations). They illustrate this compatibility with, among others, the example of social-network theory.

4

Why So Much Consensus?

4.1 Individuals as Collectives of Collectives

So let us free the individual agent from the confines of traditional rationality, through which he is transformed—some might say caricatured—as a
monolithic and immovable decision-maker, and explore the possibility that his
preferences may also be the result of a process of aggregation. This conjures
up a balanced social space, in which individuals and collective entities play
symmetrical roles: each one operates at the junction of a set of relationships
and draws on these connections to forge an opinion and make decisions.

4.1.1 The Dual Network

The most appropriate concept with which to represent this dual perspective
of society is that of the network (Breiger, 1974), whose nodes represent both
individual and collective agents, i.e. for the purposes of this essay, shareholders
and the groups they form. Combined, these nodes and the links between them
form a graph, denoted as $\mathcal{G}$. One link connects individual i to collective j if
consumer i is a shareholder in firm j.

Imagine a simple scenario of an economy comprising two firms, A and B,
and three consumers, 1, 2 and 3. Now assume that consumer 1 inherits the full
ownership of firm A, and consumers 2 and 3 inherit firm B. The shareholding
network established by these initial portfolios $\bar{\theta}$ is represented by Graph $\mathcal{G}_1$
(Fig. 4.1). We can see that it contains two separate components, one performed
by the couplet $\{1, A\}$, and one by the triplet $\{2, 3, B\}$.

If we now assume that after trading on the financial market all three
consumers become shareholders in both firms, the new shareholding network
established by these subsequent portfolios θ is represented by Graph $\mathcal{G}_2$
(Fig. 4.2). This graph now contains just one component, and the economy is
completely connected.

*Democracy, the Market, and the Firm: How the Interplay between Trading and Voting Fosters Political Stability and
Economic Efficiency.* Hervé Crès and Mich Tvede, Oxford University Press. © Hervé Crès and Mich Tvede 2021.
DOI: 10.1093/oso/9780192894731.003.0005

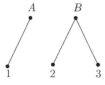

Fig. 4.1 Graph $\mathcal{G}_1$

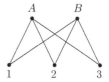

Fig. 4.2 Graph $\mathcal{G}_2$

This is a flat representation of the market. Instead of depicting the individual level of consumers and, 'above' that, the collective level of the firms, where decisions are made by aggregating the lower level, it depicts one single level and the aggregation of all the nodes in the network (Latour, 2005). Here, the individuals themselves become collectives, or rather collectives of collectives, which explains the dual understanding of the shareholding network: shareholders are linked to one another through the groups they form, and these groups are linked to one another through the shareholders they have in common.

4.1.2 Reciprocal Aggregation

A process of aggregation is at work at each node of the graph, transforming the value vectors. Imagine for a moment a specific shareholding network: consider firm j and its set of shareholders $\mathcal{I}_j \subset \mathcal{I}$. The decision-making process within the firm produces value vector ∇_j for firm j by aggregation, via aggregator $\mathcal{E}$, of the value vectors $(\nabla_{ij})_{i \in \mathcal{I}_j}$ of its different shareholders. The aggregator $\mathcal{E}$ represents all kinds of possible decision-making processes, from voting to vote-trading and from deliberations to log-rolling.

The value vector ∇_{ij} is itself a clearly defined object, for example by equations (1.3), (1.5) or (1.4). It reflects how the specific interests of consumer i are expressed within firm j. In this respect, it is a 'collectivization' of the value vector ∇_i.

So far, there is nothing new to any of this.

Now consider consumer i and the set of firms $\mathcal{J}_i \subset \mathcal{J}$ in which he holds shares. The (new) hypothesis is that an internal process of revision takes place within the shareholder in symmetry with the previous one, producing value vector ∇_i by aggregation (via aggregator $\mathcal{S}$) of the value vectors $(\nabla_{ji})_{j \in \mathcal{J}_i}$ of the different groups to which consumer i belongs. Here ∇_{ji} represents the value vector of firm j in the decision-making environment of consumer i—we will see this in more detail in the following sections. In this respect, it is an 'individualization' of the value vector ∇_j.[1]

Overall, this notion of reciprocal aggregation can be represented by the following diagram, in which aggregators $\mathcal{E}$ and $\mathcal{S}$ form a loop:

$$
\begin{array}{ccc}
(\nabla_i)_i & \overset{\text{collectivization}}{\longrightarrow} & (\nabla_{ij})_{ij} \\[2mm]
\mathcal{S} \uparrow & & \downarrow \mathcal{E} \\[2mm]
(\nabla_{ji})_{ij} & \underset{\text{individualization}}{\longleftarrow} & (\nabla_j)_j
\end{array}
$$

whose fixed points are the system's equilibria.

4.1.3 The Pareto Principle

At this stage, the idea is to be as flexible as possible about the properties that aggregators $\mathcal{E}$ and $\mathcal{S}$ must have. The only hypothesis so far is that they respect the Pareto principle. This was discussed in length in Chapter 2 (see Definition 2.1), where it was applied at the collective level. In this chapter, it is applied indifferently at the collective and individual levels, although in an even milder way at the latter level. Consider a node n in the graph, individual or collective, it makes no difference. The Pareto principle establishes that if all the neighboring nodes around n agree that plan a is at least as good as plan b, and at least one neighboring node considers a to be better than b, then node n must also consider a to be better than b. To put it simply, the Pareto principle establishes that each n comes round to the opinion of its neighbors when they all agree. If the neighboring nodes do not all agree, then the principle does not say anything.

The image of a criminal trial jury is once again useful to illustrate the Pareto principle (at the individual level). Consider a juror who must establish whether

---

[1] A similar principle was adopted in the Arrow- and Lindahl-type models (1969 and 1958 respectively) to internalize consumption externalities or public goods by the market: each 'public' consumption x_j is 'individualized' into a 'private' consumption x_{ji} specific to individual i. The aggregation mechanism operates via a personalized price p_{ji}, which only applies to consumer i, who, on the basis of this price, makes a collective consumption demand x_{ji}; ultimately, prices adjust such that the markets clear: the individualized consumption demand must coincide with the public consumption supply in accordance with the equation $x_{ji} = x_j$. See Crès (1996).

a suspect is guilty or not. Imagine she is serving on several juries which are all hearing the same trial and *all* decide that the suspect is not guilty. Is it not likely that such collective unanimity (all collectives agree—which is not the same as unanimity within each collective entity) would influence the individual opinion of our hypothetical juror, whatever it is? The hypothesis here is that in such circumstances the juror could bow to the unanimity of the juries' collective judgments and convince herself that the suspect is not guilty.

Our results hold with an even weaker version of the Pareto principle at the individual level, for which *the individual keeps considering her own initial preference when aggregating*: take a shareholder comparing plan a and plan b; suppose that all assemblies in which she sits consider a is at least as good as b, *and she also does*; suppose moreover that at least one of these assemblies, *or she*, considers a is better than b; then she considers a is better than b. Hence a great deal of *reflexivity* is kept in the aggregation mechanism at the individual level, in particular *it cannot entail a reversal of an individual preference, but only (maybe) a strengthening of it.*

The central message in this chapter (Theorem 4.1) is that an alignment of value vectors results from the Pareto principle. In the system's stable states, within a given assembly the value vectors are all identical, in line with the CAC 40 GAs discussed throughout this essay. Furthermore, the value vectors from one assembly to another are identical if they have shareholders in common. We are very much wading through the realm of single thought.

4.1.4 Thinking Inside and Outside the Box

There is simple mathematical reasoning underpinning this finding of convergence towards single thought. To understand it, let us return to the simple example of an economy with two firms, A and B, but this time with two consumers, 1 and 2, each a shareholder in both firms. If the decision-making mechanism within firm A satisfies the Pareto principle, then Proposition 2.1 implies that its judgment, as represented by value vector ∇_A, lies within the cone of value vectors ∇_1 and ∇_2; idem for firm B and ∇_B (see Fig. 4.1).

Reciprocally, if consumer 1's decision-making process satisfies the Pareto principle, then Proposition 4.1 (below) implies that his value vector ∇_1 must lie within the cone of value vectors ∇_A and ∇_B, where ∇'_1 represents a new judgment; idem for consumer 2 and ∇_2, where ∇'_2 represents a new judgment (see Fig. 4.2). Under a further iteration, ∇_A and ∇_B must also lie within the cone of the new value vectors ∇'_1 and ∇'_2, and so on. Successive iterations

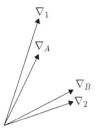

Fig. 4.3
Illustration of
Proposition 2.1

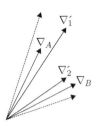

Fig. 4.4
Illustration of
Proposition 4.1

reveal that the only way for ∇_A and ∇_B to be within the cone of ∇_1 and ∇_2, and at the same time for ∇_1 and ∇_2 to be within the cone of ∇_A and ∇_B, is for all four value vectors to be aligned.

In other words, Proposition 2.1 tells us that a collective of individuals cannot think 'outside the box' defined by its members, as this box is determined by the judgments of those members, in this case the cone of vectors ∇_1 and ∇_2. When applied to an individual, Proposition 4.1 tells us reciprocally that the individual only thinks within the box determined by the collective entities to which he belongs, i.e. ∇_A and ∇_B, which the expression 'thinking inside the box' reflects with a simple image and, as we see here, a certain mathematical accuracy. By extending the metaphor, Theorem 4.1 reveals that because collective entities only think inside the box defined by their members, if individuals themselves only think inside the box defined by the collective entities to which they belong, then the self-referential serpent bites its own tail and ultimately all parties can only be thinking the same thing.

We will now return to the axiom underpinning this incapacity to think outside the box, the Pareto principle, and discuss its scope and how realistic it is.

4.1.5 Is the Pareto Principle Desirable?

There is nothing unsettling about asserting that aggregator ε respects the Pareto principle. After all, only considerations relating to an opportunity that is *extrinsic* to the aggregation mechanism could justify imposing a decision within a collective entity that runs counter to the unanimous opinion of its members. Also, as the reader was reminded after Definition 2.1, the standard argument for profit maximization (on a perfect and complete market, without any kind of externality) already stems from a simple form of the unanimity rule: all shareholders agree on maximizing their own respective income, therefore they unanimously vote for profit maximization, hence firms *should* implement a profit-maximizing production plan. We are here on very consensual ground.

But the same is not true of aggregator S. For what about *free will*? Is it not sometimes salutary for an individual to be in the right—or even in the wrong—when all those around him hold the opposite stance? Of course it is. Theorem 4.1 gives us proof of this: if the Pareto principle is imposed on individuals, all it takes is for the economy to be fully connected for single thought to reign, a state of affairs that is hardly desirable.

This chapter's contribution is easily conducive to a normative reading. Because it is difficult to contest that a form of aggregation is at work at every decision-making node, and because it is at the very least unusual to reject the hypothesis that aggregator $\mathcal{E}$ satisfies the Pareto principle, then the only controversial hypothesis preserving us from single thought is that aggregator S satisfies the Pareto principle (with reflexivity). And so if single thought is perceived as a danger, or as a threat, then individuals clearly need to be encouraged to think outside the box, and therefore never to be intimidated by the unanimous opinions of established authorities.

If on the other hand single thought is perceived as a positive thing, one that eliminates conflicts and allows society to achieve its destiny—and, in the case of the CAC 40 firms, to hasten the success of their strategies—then individuals need to be steered towards modesty and encouraged to fall in line with the unanimous opinions of the collectives to which they are affiliated, when this unanimity occurs.

4.1.6 Is the Pareto Principle Realistic?

Once again, applying the Pareto principle to collective decisions requires little precaution. Here, we will focus on its application to individual decisions, which runs counter to the prevailing economic view asserting the immutability of individual preferences.

However, we will see that applying the Pareto principle to individuals does not necessarily require a profound revision of their preferences, indeed no revision at all: in the case of production externalities, for example, the Pareto principle comes in the form of a simple adjustment to the individual's share portfolio, in a way that is completely compatible with the logic of traditional economic analysis (see Section 4.3). In the case of an incomplete market, by contrast, the Pareto principle means adjusting the preferences of the individual agent, but we insist: one that does not entail a reversal of an individual preference, but only (maybe) a strengthening of it.

There is more: we will see that in the model of expected utility, such a strengthening does not necessarily involve altering the *tastes* of the consumer, but simply updating his *beliefs* about the likelihoods of the various future economic scenarios, a principle that is universally accepted in classical economic thinking (see Section 4.4).

In the interest of honesty, a caveat is needed here: in the dominant economic analysis, beliefs are updated when an individual acquires new information based on hard facts and rooted in an objective reality, for example in relation to the price of a transaction, a competitor's technology, or a regulatory text. For the case we are interested in, the new information is implicitly conveyed by collective judgments about the likelihood of possible future scenarios. It may not be as subjective as individual feelings about the issue, and can hardly be likened to a cork bobbing about on the seas, but it might be said to float nonetheless, like a vessel perhaps. To extend this metaphor: the greater the number of members in the collective entity, the larger—and therefore more stable—the vessel. Although we may not be on the terra firma of physical information, collective judgments about future possible scenarios nonetheless provide information that is to be taken seriously, particularly in the world of economics, when mere anticipations often become reality.

4.1.7 Making a Virtue of Necessity

This presents us with a third argument in favor of the Pareto principle, to be added to *affectio societatis* and the intersubjective—if not objective—nature of collective decisions, both outlined earlier in this essay. This argument is that there may be excellent reasons—if not a rationale in its own right—for adapting to the unanimous views of the groups to which we belong, or simply for adopting those views outright.

The reasoning for this is as follows. Given that these views are unanimous, there is every chance they will ultimately be imposed, thereby generating a state of affairs that must be dealt with. It is reasonable for an individual to adapt to such inevitable circumstances, just as it is reasonable for an individual investor to purchase those assets whose value he expects to soar. This is true regardless of the information underpinning his belief, even if it is anecdotal or absurd.[2]

---

[2] An accumulation of individual reasons does not necessarily lead to collective reason. The financial markets often provide proof of this. If, upon leaving the house for work in the morning, a trader in the City sees the sun shining and says to himself, "Oh! The sun is shining on London today, so the market is set to rise"—because he knows this to be true, as absurd as it may seem to him (after all, why on earth

If all of the firms in which an individual invests opt for a certain type of strategy, based on their shared belief about future states of the world—we insist: a belief with which our investor does not disagree—then one of two things must happen: either he stands firm, in which case he could 'vote with his feet,' as the expression goes, and sell his investments, thereby leaving these collective entities; or he decides to stay on, in which case he may as well embrace the future with peace of mind and adhere to the unanimous vision of these firms, in other words climb on board.

It appears to be perfectly reasonable to revise one's beliefs in order to improve one's welfare. Changing one's tastes for the same purpose does not seem any less reasonable. This points to a certain strength, that of 'making a virtue of necessity'—the *amor fati* of the Stoics (Elster, 1983). We will return to this in more detail in Chapter 5.

Section 4.2 introduces the notion of reciprocal aggregation equilibrium in the generic scenario of a failing market. This scenario is applied to production externalities in Section 4.3, to the case of an incomplete market in Sections 4.4 and 4.5, and to the case of imperfect competition in Section 4.6. In the first two cases, we will see that the notion of equilibrium is even more general than in traditional general equilibrium models, but does not require anything which is not classic: in the presence of production externalities, it requires portfolio transactions (although in a static context); on an incomplete market, it requires the beliefs of agents to be updated.

4.2 Reciprocal Aggregation

This section presents the generic framework of a failing market, without specifying the nature of its failure. Nor is the governance structure of the firms specified.

4.2.1 The Pareto Principle at the Individual Level

We will hypothesize that, when forming their value vectors, shareholders cannot overlook the value vectors of the collective entities with which they

would cloud cover over London that day have an impact on the value of the assets traded across the world?)—then reason tells him to buy, or he will lose out on an opportunity to make an easy profit. And if all his fellow traders anticipate the same thing, then they all buy and the market does indeed rise as anticipated (see Hirshleifer & Shumway, 2003). And if he abstains from buying because he finds this general fervor absurd, no matter how much he pleads for collective reason, he risks losing his job. On the market it is rare to be right and for everyone else to be wrong; or at least this is only possible in the long term, but one must first survive until then.

are affiliated, and in particular those of the firms in which they invest. They take them into account one way or the other and use them to update or adapt their own value vectors. In short, individuals aggregate collective value vectors, just as collectives aggregate individual value vectors. And when evaluating a proposed change Δy to the production plan of a firm in which he has invested, shareholder i takes into account the $\#\mathcal{J}_i$ potentially different evaluations of the firms in which he has a stake, as represented by the value vectors $(\nabla_j)_{j \in \mathcal{J}_i}$. This naturally points to the dual version of Definition 2.1, which defines the Pareto principle when it operates between individuals within a collective entity: Definition 4.1 defines the (reflexive) Pareto principle when it operates between collective entities in the inner thoughts of an individual.

Definition 4.1 *For value vectors* $((\nabla_i)_{i \in \mathcal{I}}, (\nabla_j)_{j \in \mathcal{J}})$:

- ∇_i *respects the (reflexive) Pareto principle if for all* $\Delta y \in \mathbb{R}^\ell$, $\nabla_i \cdot \Delta y \geq 0$ *and* $\nabla_j \cdot \Delta y \geq 0$ *for every* $j \in \mathcal{J}_i$, *with at least one strict inequality, implies that* $\nabla_i \cdot \Delta y > 0$.
- $(\nabla_i)_{i \in \mathcal{I}}$ *is Pareto stable if* ∇_i *respects the Pareto principle for every* j.

This principle is milder than the version for collectives in Definition 2.1, since it puts even fewer constraints on the aggregation process. First, as usual with the Pareto principle, a shareholder is affected only when the firms in which she invests *all* make the same judgment.[3] Second, and this is the reflexive part, a shareholder is affected only when she does not disagree with this unanimous judgment. Third, she is affected only at the margin, to the extent that indifference becomes a preference. By no means does it entail a reversal of a preference.

Despite this fundamental difference, the dual version of Proposition 2.1 follows.

Proposition 4.1 *Let* $((\nabla_i)_{i \in \mathcal{I}}, (\nabla_j)_{j \in \mathcal{J}})$ *be value vectors.* ∇_i *respects the Pareto principle if and only if* $\nabla_i \in \angle^+(\nabla_j)_{j \in \mathcal{J}_i}$.

Here, ∇_i is a mean of the value vectors of the firms in which consumer i holds shares. Let us return briefly to the geometric interpretation of this result: the cone $\angle^+$ delimits the space of collective judgments; Proposition 4.1 asserts that respect for the Pareto principle, even in this reflexive form, means the shareholder is incapable of moving beyond the boundaries. If $\angle^+$ is the 'box' of

---

[3] If the shareholder invests in only one firm, this first argument is weak. But we know that, in general equilibrium, it is generically the case that portfolios are well diversified.

collective opinions, the individual is unable to think outside the box. But since collective judgments themselves stem from individual opinions, there is a self-referential dynamic at work. And if the network of affiliations is sufficiently interconnected, then all individuals and all collectives are at equilibrium with the same value vectors. This is formalized in the following section.

4.2.2 Stable States and Shareholder Alignment

As indicated in the introduction, the dual network of affiliations generated by a list of portfolios θ can be represented by a bipartite graph $\mathcal{G}(\theta)$ in which the nodes represent consumers and firms, with consumer i and firm j connected when $\theta_{ij} > 0$. The graph $\mathcal{G}$ has a certain number of connected components, also known as clusters.

Definition 4.2 *For a list of portfolios θ, a cluster is a non-empty subset of consumers and firms $\mathcal{C} \subset \mathcal{I} \cup \mathcal{J}$ such that*

$$(\cup_{i \in \mathcal{C}} \mathcal{J}_i) \cup (\cup_{j \in \mathcal{C}} \mathcal{I}_j) = \mathcal{C},$$

and

$$\mathcal{D} \subset \mathcal{C} \text{ and } (\cup_{i \in \mathcal{D}} \mathcal{J}_i) \cup (\cup_{j \in \mathcal{D}} \mathcal{I}_j) = \mathcal{D} \Rightarrow \mathcal{D} = \mathcal{C} \text{ or } \mathcal{D} = \emptyset.$$

Let $((\bar{U}_i, \bar{x}_i, \bar{\theta}_i)_{i \in \mathcal{I}}, (g_j)_{j \in \mathcal{J}})$ define the economy. Let $U = (U_1, \ldots, U_I)$.

Definition 4.3 *An economic state (U, θ, x, y) is a list of utility functions and portfolios and an allocation. A state (U, θ, x, y) is stable if $(\nabla_j(y_j))_{j \in \mathcal{J}}$ and $(\nabla_i(U_i, x_i))_{i \in \mathcal{I}}$ are Pareto stable.*

If the graph of affiliations $\mathcal{G}(\theta)$ is connected, in a stable state the firms and shareholders are all aligned. This is the 'single thought theorem.'

Theorem 4.1 *Consider (U, θ, x, y) to be a stable state at which graph $\mathcal{G}(\theta)$ is connected; then there is $\nabla \in \mathbb{S}^\ell$ such that $\nabla_i(U_i, x_i) = \nabla_j(y_j) = \nabla$ for every i and j.*

If the graph $\mathcal{G}(\theta)$ is not connected, alignment will occur within each cluster which is an interpretation of the unanimity observed in CAC40 GAs.

Corollary 4.1 *Consider* (U, θ, x, y) *to be a stable state; then for each cluster* C *there is* $\nabla_c \in \mathbb{S}^\ell$ *such that* $\nabla_i(U_i, x_i) = \nabla_j(y_j) = \nabla_c$ *for every* $i, j \in C$.

One immediate consequence of alignment is allocation efficiency.

Corollary 4.2 *Consider* (U, θ, x, y) *to be a stable state at which graph* $\mathcal{G}(\theta)$ *is connected; then the allocation* (x, y) *is efficient.*

Everything is now in place to suggest a notion of general equilibrium based on the reciprocal aggregation hypothesis.

4.2.3 Reciprocal Aggregation Equilibrium

In the Walrasian concept of market equilibrium, consumers exchange their endowments $\bar{x}$ for their optimal bundles x^* in respect of market prices p, as we saw in Sections 1.2, 1.4 and 1.5, such that, based on fundamental characteristics $(\bar{U}, \bar{\theta}, \bar{x})$, an equilibrium is reflected in a list $(\bar{U}, \bar{\theta}, x^*)$. When the financial market is open, consumers further exchange their initial portfolios $\bar{\theta}$ for optimal portfolios θ^*—which finance x^*—in respect of asset prices q, as we saw in Section 1.3, such that an equilibrium is reflected in a list $(\bar{U}, \theta^*, x^*)$.

When applied at the individual level, the Pareto principle requires transactions that go beyond these traditional limits. In the presence of production externalities, transactions relate not only to bundles but also to portfolios; and in the context of an incomplete market, they relate not only to bundles and portfolios but also to preferences. For the purposes of simplifying the notation, in this section the characteristics of an equilibrium will be denoted by (U^*, θ^*, x^*) and all prices by p.

A notion of (even more) general equilibrium can be proposed based on three pillars: individual optimization, market clearing, and the stability of reciprocal aggregation. It combines the notion of a stable state (Definition 4.3) and that of market equilibrium (Definition 1.4). Classical general equilibrium analysis is based on the first two of these pillars, and sometimes on the stability of aggregation at the collective level. Requiring the stability of aggregation at the individual level further broadens the concept of general equilibrium and brings more complex transactions into play.

Definition 4.4 *A **reciprocal aggregation equilibrium** $(p^*, U^*, \theta^*, x^*, y^*)$ is a price vector and a stable state such that (p^*, x^*, y^*) is a market equilibrium.*

These equilibria provide an interpretation of the broad consensus observed in the firms of the CAC 40. Although the equilibrium portfolios θ^* do not necessarily give rise to a connected graph, all agents, individual and collective, are aligned within a single cluster. And shareholders within a single GA are by definition in the same cluster.

4.3 Internal Choice Consistency

In the presence of production externalities, the Pareto principle at the individual level can go through portfolio transactions, and in ways that are perfectly compatible with standard competition analysis, except to say that the mindset underpinning these transactions is not the traditional need for insurance and savings—there is no such need in a static economy—but rather the need to preserve the internal consistency of choices.

Let (U, θ, x, y) be an economic state, where $y = f(a)$. For every firm there is a virtual portfolio θ_j that supports plan y_j insofar as $\nabla_j = \Xi_j \theta_j$. An immediate corollary of Propositions 2.1 and 4.1 follows.

Corollary 4.3 *In a stable state:* $\theta_j \in \angle^+(\theta_i)_{i \in I_j}$ *and* $\theta_i \in \angle^+(\theta_j)_{j \in J_i}$.

The aggregation that takes place within consumer i gives rise to a *posterior* portfolio, typically differing from the initial portfolio $\bar{\theta}_i$.

4.3.1 Absence of Arbitrage

Therefore, considering that assets are traded on the market, and given price vectors p for goods, q for assets, and decisions a for firms, consumer i chooses his optimal bundle from the budget set

$$B_i(p, q, a) = \left\{ x_i \mid p \cdot x_i \leq p \cdot (\bar{x}_i + Y(a)\theta_i) + q \cdot (\bar{\theta}_i - \theta_i) \right\}.$$

It is inevitable that the posterior portfolio θ_i will be chosen in order to maximize wealth: $p \cdot \bar{x}_i + q \cdot \bar{\theta}_i + \sum_j \theta_{ij}(p \cdot f_j(a) - q_j)$. The standard conditions for the absence of arbitrage therefore imply

$$q_j = p \cdot f_j(a),$$

such that wealth is independent of θ_i, and $B_i(p, q, a)$ is reduced to the traditional set: $B_i(p, q, a) = B_i(p, f(a))$ of Section 1.4.

In the absence of aggregation at the individual level, the financial markets are clearly redundant and therefore of no use. But if consumers can trade their shares at prices that guarantee the absence of arbitrage, then they are free to choose posterior portfolios θ that support their value vectors: consumer i chooses θ_i such that $\nabla_{ij} = \Xi_j \theta_i$. And at equilibrium the market clears: $\sum_i \theta_i = 1_J$.

Consumers behave in line with the canons of competition analysis not only on the commodities market but also on the securities market. Portfolio transactions are driven by internal choice consistency.

4.3.2 Existence of a Reciprocal Aggregation Equilibrium

For economy $((\bar{U}_i, \bar{x}_i, \bar{\theta}_i)_{i \in I}, (g_j)_{j \in J})$ the existence of a reciprocal aggregation equilibrium can be obtained readily.

Remark 4.1 *For all Walrasian equilibria (p^*, x^*, y^*) with efficient internalization of externalities, there exists θ^* such that $(p^*, \bar{U}, \theta^*, x^*, y^*)$ is a reciprocal aggregation equilibrium.*

The existence of a reciprocal aggregation equilibrium is thus established, and stems from the standard arguments. The equilibria described in Remark 4.1 are Pareto-optimal since the graph of affiliations $\mathcal{G}(\theta^*)$ is connected. This is not necessarily true of all reciprocal aggregation equilibria.

4.4 Consistent Beliefs

In the context of an incomplete market, at the individual level the Pareto principle requires a change in preferences. However, this does not necessarily imply a change in individual tastes, if we follow the precept *gustibus non est disputandum* (Stigler & Becker, 1977); all that is needed is simply to update one's beliefs about the likelihood of the various economic scenarios occurring in the future. We will now look at the form this takes in the case of consumers maximizing an expected utility function, with subjective probabilities.

4.4.1 The Expected Utility Framework

Consumer i holds a subjective belief that takes the form of a probability vector $\pi_i \in \mathbb{S}^\ell$ in relation to the ℓ states of the world as of date 1; he is represented by an elementary utility function $u_i : \mathbb{R} \to \mathbb{R}$ that accounts for his tastes. Let $\vec{u}_i(x_i) = (u_i(x_i^s))_s$ denote the vector of utility levels in each state of the world, such that

$$U_i(x_i) = \pi_i \cdot \vec{u}_i(x_i) = \sum_s \pi_i^s u_i(x_i^s).$$

In this section, u_i is fixed but the belief π_i can be updated.

This framework is particularly well suited to the type of uncertainty that firms face. They invest based on prospects whose likelihoods are extremely difficult to establish with complete objectivity. For example, it would be a clever analyst who could tell you the objective probability of the price of a barrel of oil settling above a given threshold over the next five years. Beliefs can be no more than subjective and moldable. It is widely accepted that they can be revised based on credible information. This essay puts forward the hypothesis that during transactions agents infer the beliefs of other agents based on the opinions they express and the choices they make, and they decide to revise their own beliefs in light of this information as part of a mechanism that is constrained by only one axiom: the Pareto principle.

4.4.2 Updating Beliefs

If firm j produces plan y_j, the shareholders infer the value vector $\nabla_j(y_j)$ used to maximize profits (see Lemma 1.1). From this value vector, they deduce the probability vector implicitly used by firm j.

For the purposes of clarity, suppose for a moment that the agents are risk-neutral. $\nabla_j^{\|}(y_j)$ is then interpreted as the probability vector π_j used by firm j to calculate expected profit. From Proposition 4.1, there are $\nu_{ij} > 0$ such that

$$\pi_i = \sum_{j \in \mathcal{J}_i} \nu_{ij} \pi_j. \tag{4.1}$$

This is the model proposed by DeGroot (1974) for the formation of beliefs on a graph, where shareholder i attributes the weight ν_{ij} to the belief of firm j; the weight ν_{ij} here reveals the authority carried by firm j's board of directors in the eyes of shareholder i, or the degree of loyalty which shareholder i feels towards firm j, or a combination of the two.

This interpretation can be transposed onto the case of risk-averse agents. Faced with a value vector ∇, consumer i calculates the underlying probability vector in the universe of his own consumption, in accordance with the hypothesis of competitive belief perception.[4] His own value vector is

$$D_{x_i} U_i(\pi_i, x_i) = \left(\pi_i^1 u_i'(x_i^1), \cdots, \pi_i^\ell u_i'(x_i^\ell)\right)$$

up to normalization. The marginal utility $u_i'(x_i^s)$ is the value for consumer i of one unit of the commodity in state s without regard to its probability. In the spirit of competition analysis, we assume the agent has no information about the marginal utilities of other consumers. Furthermore, the firms do not have preferences. Faced with a value vector ∇, consumer i therefore uses his own marginal utilities to extract the probability vector underlying ∇.

To do so is mere child's play. Given x_i, the ℓ vectors

$$e_i^s(x_i) = (0, \cdots, 0, u_i'(x_i^s), 0, \cdots, 0), \ 1 \le s \le \ell,$$

form a basis for $\mathbb{R}^\ell$ (since $u_i'(x_i^s) \ne 0$). Within this basis, the coordinates of $D_{x_i} U_i(\pi_i, x_i)$ are π_i. Similarly, there is just one $\pi \in \mathbb{S}^\ell$ such that the coordinates of ∇ are π up to normalization. This can be expressed as $\pi(x_i, \nabla)$.

4.4.3 Absence of Arbitrage

At market equilibrium, all consumers agree on how to evaluate transfers in the asset span $\langle Y \rangle$; i.e. by Lemma 1.4, $\nabla_i^T Y$ is collinear to q^*: individual value vectors lie in the linear subspace guaranteeing no arbitrage. Thanks to the Pareto principle at the collective level (Proposition 2.1) the same applies to the firms' value vectors. In turn, any update of beliefs respecting the Pareto principle at the individual level therefore involves a change in the value vectors in this same sub-space. As a result, the notion of reciprocal aggregation equilibrium only involves belief updates in the absence of arbitrage: it is impossible to combine an update of beliefs with a financial transfer in a way that increases the level of utility.

---

[4] This hypothesis is inspired by the *competitive price perception* hypothesis proposed by Grossman & Hart (1979).

So, combined with the notion of market equilibrium, reciprocal aggregation is a neutral principle when it comes to welfare. Here, as in the case of redundant portfolio transactions in the previous section, consumers behave in line with the canons of competition analysis not only on the commodities and securities markets, but also on the 'market of beliefs.' Belief updates are driven by internal choice consistency and do not involve any change in utility. In the absence of update costs, and if we accept the traditional hypothesis that prices adjust to guarantee the absence of arbitrage, there is nothing to oppose such updates.

4.4.4 Existence of Reciprocal Aggregation Equilibria

A reciprocal aggregation equilibrium $(q^*, U^*, \theta^*, x^*, y^*)$ is such that (q^*, x^*, y^*) is a market equilibrium both for $\bar{U}$ and U^*. The transaction can therefore precede, be concomitant with or consecutive to the update of beliefs.

One important remark to which we will return is that reciprocal aggregation equilibria are indeterminate. Any value vector can be imposed on the economy, even in the context of expected utility.

Remark 4.2 *Let* $\left((\bar{\pi}_i \cdot \vec{u}_i, \bar{x}_i, \bar{\theta}_i)_{i \in \mathcal{I}}, (g_j)_{j \in \mathcal{J}} \right)$ *be an economy with expected utilities. For a value vector* $\nabla \in \mathbb{S}^\ell$, *there is a reciprocal aggregation equilibrium at which all value vectors equal* ∇.

The equilibria described in Remark 4.2 are Pareto-optimal, even though the affiliation graph $\mathcal{G}(\theta^*)$ might not be connected.

One sees that at reciprocal aggregation equilibria, even if the value vectors are collinear and in the same direction, the beliefs typically differ from one consumer to the other. They then agree on how to manage the firm, but not on the probability of the states of the world. Therefore, it could be argued that the alignment described in Theorem 4.1 and Corollary 4.1 is 'spurious' (Mongin, 1997).

4.5 A Spurious Consensus?

The single thought theorem is underpinned by a thesis, and a hypothesis. The thesis is that when it comes to public choices, individual decisions are not implacably determined by an immutable objective function that is impermeable to all external influence, but on the contrary the fruit of a process of aggregation that is fed by the links between the individual and the public sphere. The hypothesis is that this process of aggregation obeys the Pareto principle. This may not be the most conventional hypothesis with respect to the dominant economic thinking, but, as we have seen, there is nothing revolutionary about interpreting Equation (4.1) as a simple update of beliefs, as understood by DeGroot. The import of this finding relates as much to the dual perspective and the notion of reciprocal aggregation as to the strength of the hypotheses. One of the most notable consequences of the single thought theorem is that when the economy is fully connected, the combined impact of the market and of reciprocal aggregation is efficient.

4.5.1 Single Thought and Economic Efficiency

In the case of production externalities, if we accept the thesis outlined in Section 4.3 about how the Pareto principle works at the individual level, then single thought and market efficiency become one and the same concept: the Pareto principle compels individual investors to readjust their asset portfolio in the interest of choice consistency; in doing so, they all end up buying the market portfolio and thereby promote the efficient allocation of resources. But in that case, is it the market that is efficient, or is it the desire for internal consistency among individual agents incapable of thinking outside the box determined by firms?

In the case of an incomplete market, efficiency is ultimately characterized by the alignment of value vectors. This alignment comes about through trading on the market and through the reciprocal revision of beliefs, those of individuals and collectives. If the financial structure is complete, there is no need for aggregation. But inversely, if there is no limit to aggregation, i.e. where the beliefs of investors are completely malleable and the Pareto principle can apply without constraint, then there is *no need for a financial market*, a troubling prospect.

However, it is useful to have the following hierarchy of changes in mind: first, consumers trade on the market; next, if trading does not align their value vectors within those of the collectives to which they affiliate, then they revise their beliefs.[5] Thereby, a balanced reading of the alternative appears, namely that the financial market and reciprocal aggregation complement and reinforce one another. Indeed, the more the market is complete, the less aggregation distorts individual beliefs; and the more individual beliefs are malleable, the less the financial market is necessary.

---

[5] Finally, if neither trading nor changing beliefs align their value vectors within that of the collectives to which they affiliate, then they change their tastes—a step that could be needed if preferences are not of the expected-utility type, or in the case of imperfect competition (see Section 4.6).

4.5.2 The Pareto Principle and Spurious Unanimity

On an incomplete market, unanimity in shareholder groups may be spurious (Mongin, 1997), insofar as it may be based on a combination of different beliefs ($\pi_i \neq \pi_{i'}$) and different tastes ($u_i \neq u_{i'}$) that compensate for one another. Shareholders may have opposing beliefs and opposing tastes, but these cancel each other out and seal a kind of alliance of opposites; so they may be unanimous, but for the 'wrong' reasons. It would follow that the Pareto principle is not always very convincing.

Suppose for example there are two possible future states of the world, state 1 and state 2, and two shareholders, named 1 and 2 for convenience, both of whom own a firm in equal shares. Now suppose shareholder 1 considers state 1 highly improbable: $\pi_1^1 = \epsilon$, where ϵ is very small, but in terms of his tastes he would far prefer to consume in state 1, with a very large marginal utility (relative to state 2), equal to $1/\epsilon$. This gives us the following belief and taste parameters:

$$\pi_1 = \begin{pmatrix} \epsilon \\ 1 - \epsilon \end{pmatrix} \text{ and } \vec{u}_1' = \begin{pmatrix} 1/\epsilon \\ 1 \end{pmatrix}.$$

Now suppose it is the exact opposite for shareholder 2:

$$\pi_2 = \begin{pmatrix} 1 - \epsilon \\ \epsilon \end{pmatrix} \text{ and } \vec{u}_2' = \begin{pmatrix} 1 \\ 1/\epsilon \end{pmatrix}.$$

The two shareholders have opposing beliefs and opposing tastes, but ultimately their value vectors are almost aligned:

$$\nabla_1 = \begin{pmatrix} 1 \\ 1 - \epsilon \end{pmatrix} \text{ and } \nabla_2 = \begin{pmatrix} 1 - \epsilon \\ 1 \end{pmatrix}.$$

The cone determined by ∇_1 and ∇_2 has a sharp angle, as shown in Fig. 4.3 for the normalized value vectors $\nabla_1^{\parallel}$ and $\nabla_2^{\parallel}$; and only production plans supported by prices within this cone are stable. At the limit, when ϵ tends towards 0, their value vectors are aligned: $\nabla_1 = \nabla_2 = (1, 1)$, and only the production plan supported by price $(1,1)$ is stable.

In terms of collective decisions, the Pareto principle has always been considered a minimal hypothesis. One might describe it as the ultimate defense against conservatism. And as well founded as the critique of spurious unanimity may be, it is difficult to imagine operational procedures that would make

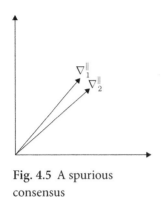

Fig. 4.5 A spurious consensus

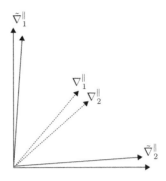

Fig. 4.6 A wide divergence

it possible to distinguish between spurious and non-spurious unanimity (Crès & Tvede, 2018). In any case, it is worth pointing out that with regard to the interpretation proposed in Section 4.4, this critique is not valid when it comes to applying the Pareto principle at the individual level. Each individual uses the same price vector to 'read' the beliefs of firms, and so the Pareto principle applies based on the same tastes: those of the individual concerned.

4.5.3 Alternatives to the Pareto Principle

The critique of spurious unanimity has sharpened the imagination of economists, who have proposed revisions of the Pareto principle with which to judge the appeal of an economic transaction. For example, Gilboa et al. (2014) suggest that a transaction to which all stakeholders adhere can nonetheless be contested; it is incontestable only if it remains beneficial for all stakeholders *for at least one shared belief*. Gayer et al. (2014) argue that a transaction is incontestable only if it remains beneficial for each of the beliefs held by all the different parties.

If we had to impose the Gilboa et al. (2014) criterion, and only accept a production change if it were beneficial for both shareholders subject to one shared belief $(\pi, 1 - \pi)$, then the value vectors to be taken into account in the above example would be

$$\tilde{\nabla}_1 = \begin{pmatrix} \pi/\epsilon \\ 1 - \pi \end{pmatrix} \text{ and } \tilde{\nabla}_2 = \begin{pmatrix} \pi \\ (1 - \pi)/\epsilon \end{pmatrix};$$

these form a cone with a very wide angle, as shown in Fig. 4.4 for the normalized value vectors $\tilde{\nabla}_1^{\parallel}$ and $\tilde{\nabla}_2^{\parallel}$; and at the limit, when ϵ tends towards 0, all production plans are stable. This would lead to the most absolute conservatism.

The unanimity may be spurious, but at least it allows for progress. Room for discussion but unity in action: this is the strength of the democratic centralism so dear to Lenin.

4.5.4 On the Separation between Beliefs and Tastes

Some economists nonetheless assert that it is impossible to clearly distinguish between beliefs and tastes, even when interpreting preferences represented by expected utility with subjective probabilities (Duffie, 2014). They argue that beliefs are also a matter of taste insofar as they are not purely cognitive but also affective; similarly, tastes can be reasoned and affected by all kinds of beliefs. They also correctly point out that it is impossible to distinguish between an economy in which individuals have different beliefs and tastes that are independent of the states of the world (the interpretation that prevails in this chapter), and one in which individuals have identical beliefs but tastes that depend on these states.

If we accept these critiques—and the authors are happy to do so—then the conclusions of Proposition 4.1 raise a more thorny problem of interpretation as they imply changing individual preferences, a possibility which economists have long been reluctant to contemplate but which is now the subject of an abundant literature. We will explore this in Chapter 5, but before let us illustrate the problem by investigating the case of imperfect competition.

4.6 Adaptive Preferences

In some cases, transactions on portfolios or updating of beliefs do not suffice to support the Pareto principle. Adaptive preferences have then to be envisaged. The case of a monopolistic firm offers a good illustration. Let us develop it for a slightly augmented version of the textbook scenario.[6]

---

[6] The logic of reciprocal agregation is pushed to the extreme in the case of the monopoly, as the Pareto principle imposes that individuals adopt the value vector of the monopoly. The analysis is provided here for the sake of completeness, and generalizes to the case of an oligopoly.

Consider the quadratic utility function (1.2) with weightings depending on i, $\pi_i \in \mathbb{S}_+^\ell$:

$$U_i(x_i) = \sum_{s=1}^{\ell} \pi_i^s \left(\gamma_i x_i^s - \frac{1}{2}(x_i^s)^2 \right). \tag{4.2}$$

Hence consumer i's utility function is indexed by the ℓ parameters $(\mathring{\pi}_i, \gamma_i) \in \mathbb{R}_+^\ell$, where $\mathring{\pi}_i$ denotes the $(\ell - 1)$ first coordinates of π_i (then $\pi_i^\ell = 1 - \sum_{s=1}^{\ell-1} \pi_i^s$).

The application of the (reflexive) Pareto principle implies a marginal change of the value vector ∇_i, which must 're-enter' the cone that ∇_i forms with $(\nabla_j)_{j \in \mathcal{J}_i}$. The question then becomes: is such a change feasible through a marginal change of the parameters $(\mathring{\pi}_i, \gamma_i)$? The answer is positive.

Although the firm is monopolistic, consumers still behave competitively: they do not perceive that a marginal change of their net trades will impact the prices p or the matrices Φ_j. Therefore the expression $\nabla_{ij} = \bar{\theta}_{ij} p^* - \Phi_j z_i$ implies

$$D_{(\mathring{\pi}_i, \gamma_i)} \nabla_{ij} = -\Phi_j D_{(\mathring{\pi}_i, \gamma_i)} x_i.$$

A marginal change of the parameters $(\mathring{\pi}_i, \gamma_i)$ will amend ∇_{ij} in all required directions[7] if one shows that $D_{(\mathring{\pi}_i, \gamma_i)} x_i$ has rank ℓ.

This is what the following lemma shows.

Lemma 4.1 *At equilibrium, one has*

$$x_i = \gamma_i 1_\ell - V_i(\Gamma 1_\ell - \Omega),$$

where V_i is the diagonal matrix of size ℓ where the diagonal vector is a probability vector. Moreover, the matrix $D_{(\mathring{\pi}_i, \gamma_i)} x_i$ has full rank for almost all values of $(\bar{x}_i, \bar{\theta}_i)$.

The adaptive feature of preferences which is required here to support the Pareto principle goes through a change of tastes, and not only beliefs. The following chapter reviews the issue of adaptive preferences from a wider perspective.

---

[7] Up to normalization. The matrix Φ_j has rank $\ell - 1$ at a regular equilibrium, thanks to the normalization of p. So the matrix $D_{(\mathring{\pi}_i, \gamma_i)} \nabla_{ij}$ has rank $\ell - 1$ at most.

5

Making a Virtue of Necessity

5.1 Compromise and Deliberation

That individual preferences are flexible is neither surprising nor problematic, and especially not taboo for political scientists. For many of them, following Habermas (1984), the central function of politics is to make preferences evolve with a view to forging a consensus that serves a well-understood shared interest, rather than aggregate preferences in search of a compromise between diverging and inflexible opinions and interests.[1]

The notion of reciprocal aggregation presented herein is compatible with both perspectives. In the collective entity, the Pareto principle is respected as much by a 'straight' vote, i.e. without prior discussion, as by interminable closed deliberations, provided they produce a plume of white smoke. Within the individual, the Pareto principle relates as much to the aggregation of preferences of multiple selves[2] as to the personal deliberation behind each carefully considered decision. In any case, aggregation and deliberation are two sides of the same coin and difficult to distinguish from one another in reality.

For economists, in contrast, the inflexibility of preferences has long been of cardinal importance, even though things have changed since the 1980s, mainly under the influence of psychology and behavioral economics. The formation of preferences, and therefore their essentially unstable nature, is now well established in economic thought. Section 5.2 provides a discussion of the literature and reviews the arguments that corroborate the application of the Pareto principle to individual decisions. Section 5.3 presents some of its philosophical foundations, with a focus on the notion of adaptive preferences. Section 5.4 explores the axiomatic of adaptive preferences. Sections 5.5 and 5.6 contribute to the reflection on group agency and corporate social responsibility.

---

[1] See in particular the theory of the evolution of preferences brought about by deliberation (for example Miller, 1992; Knight & Johnson, 1994; Dryzek & List, 2003).

[2] "Faust complained that he had two souls in his breast. I have a whole squabbling crowd. It goes on as in a republic." (Bismarck, quoted by Steedman & Krause, 1985).

Democracy, the Market, and the Firm: How the Interplay between Trading and Voting Fosters Political Stability and Economic Efficiency. Hervé Crès and Mich Tvede, Oxford University Press. © Hervé Crès and Mich Tvede 2021. DOI: 10.1093/oso/9780192894731.003.0006

5.2 The Flexibility of Preferences

In our search for considerations that corroborate the thesis of reciprocal aggregation and validate the Pareto principle at an individual level, one of the primary obstacles we face is the tradition in economic thought established by, among others, Becker (1976) as "the combined assumptions of maximizing behavior, market equilibrium, and stable preferences" (p. 5). This is what he described in two words as the 'economic approach.' And so the doctrine was laid down.

As already emphasized, in a context of uncertainty preferences are the concatenation of beliefs and tastes—tastes with regard to possible futures, and beliefs as to the likelihood of their occurrence, when these beliefs cannot be objectively determined. The dominant tradition does not impose the stability of beliefs—on the contrary—and the Bayesian inference is a hobby horse of economic thought. What Becker meant here by preference is that which corresponds to tastes, to the extent that one can disentangle them from beliefs.

5.2.1 Critique of the Doctrine

Becker's (1976) reluctance, and that of most economists, to accept changes in preferences was underpinned by two factors. First, "economists generally have had little to contribute [...] to the understanding of how preferences are formed" (p. 5). Second, "the assumption of stable preferences [...] prevents the analyst from succumbing to the temptation of simply postulating the required shift in preferences to explain all apparent contradictions to his predictions" (p. 5). He goes on to insist that "the economic approach does not take refuge in assertions about irrationality [...] or convenient ad hoc shifts in values (i.e. preferences)" (p. 7).[3]

A more benevolent way of putting this is that the hypothesis of stable preferences is 'parsimonious' (Dietrich & List, 2011). It is also primary, if only because it founds comparative static analysis, which is the working method par

---

[3] This leaves the question of which preferences must be stable. According to Becker (1976, p. 5): "The preferences that are assumed to be stable do not refer to market goods and services [...] but to underlying objects of choice that are produced by each household using market goods and services, their own time, and other inputs. These underlying preferences are defined over fundamental aspects of life, such as health, prestige, sensual pleasure, benevolence, or envy, that do not always bear a stable relation to market goods and services." So, under this tradition, shifts in preferences are admissible if they remain somewhat 'superficial.' In the same vein, Lancaster's theory of characteristics (1966a, 1966b) paves the way for preference changes based on structural factors rather than on new information (Dietrich & List, 2011).

excellence in economics. It suffices to explain an important part of observed phenomena, as the first part of this essay hopefully showed. As a first approach, this hypothesis is irreplaceable. But it is only a hypothesis, not a doctrine. And when facing a puzzle, as in the case of votes in CAC 40 GAs, we are bound to either reject the theory, or enlarge it by easing the constraints imposed by the strongest assumptions.

We know that the first factor in Becker's reluctance is obsolete. Under the influence of other disciplines, the social sciences or science in general, the thinking about preferences in economics has become considerably richer since the 1970s. Becker is known for having invoked the economic approach as a way to explain many social phenomena; through a shift in the pendulum, approaches borrowed from sociology, anthropology, and even biology and cognitive science have allowed us to better understand the formation and evolution of individual preferences. The rapid spread of the network method in economics over the last twenty years is a striking illustration of this (Jackson, 2008). The literature on the transmission of cultural traits is another (Bowles, 1998; Bisin & Verdier, 2001), drawing extensively on the methods and paradigms of evolutionary biology. Lastly, the noninvasive techniques of neuroimaging have facilitated the development of neuroscience, and have contributed to our understanding of shifting preferences (Izuma et al., 2010).

As for the second cause of Becker's reluctance, i.e. that an economist worthy of the title must not succumb to the temptation of ad hoc reasoning— something no-one would dispute—and must therefore refuse any reliance on shifting preferences, this is a sectarian viewpoint. Not only does it close the door on behavioral economics, but it fails to account for the normative scope of economic modeling. What if it made sense for an individual to shift preferences? And what if, furthermore, such a shift were to increase social welfare? Sometimes the model does not necessarily seek to make predictions, and the theorist is less interested in explaining reality than in imagining how to improve it.

5.2.2 Do Individual Preferences Change?

The answer is, of course, yes—if only over time. Becker himself (1976, 1996) was a prolific contributor to the literature on the acquisition of tastes over time under the influence of past behavior and experiences. Economists with an interest in industrial organization have long identified the phenomenon of 'experience goods,' whose utility can only be appreciated through usage (Nelson, 1970). Consumer theorists have modeled the formation of habits (Rozen, 2010). The notion of endogenous changes in preferences, triggered by previous consumption, has been around for half a century (von Weizsäcker, 1971; Hammond, 1976; Pollack, 1978), and the work of Kahneman & Tversky (1979) on reference-dependent preferences reveals that such changes can also take place following rational expectations (Köszegi & Rabin, 2006). All of this research points to another duality beyond that between individuals and groups: the duality between preferences and goods. What is the primal set, what is the dual set? Consumption is determined by preferences, but the reverse is also true.

Although the assumption of stable preferences may be parsimonious and should be maintained as an initial approach to explain economic phenomena, it nonetheless appears to be contradicted by many observations made in behavioral economics. One example is the supposed persistence of the 'endowment effect' (Kahneman et al., 1991). Attributing greater value to an item simply on the basis that one owns it can only be a reflection of a shift in one's preference or of reference-dependent preferences. Another example is the tendency of individuals, when asked to choose from a menu, to select the 'default option,' i.e. that which is automatically selected if they abstain from exercising their choice (Thaler & Sunstein, 2008). In the context of this essay, this bias in favor of the default option mimics the Pareto principle: if an industrial strategy is unanimously supported by all firms in the sector, it takes on a de facto status as the default option. Furthermore, when an option is imposed by all the groups to which one belongs, then adhering to it is the best way to avoid any cognitive dissonance in the future.

One well-known phenomenon that seeks to attenuate cognitive dissonance is the 'free-choice paradigm' (Brehm, 1956; Sharot et al., 2010), which tells us that having made a difficult choice between two objects or opportunities, people tend to devalue the rejected option and attach greater value to the one chosen.[4] This paradigm accredits the idea that decisions result in changed preferences. It might also remain true when the choice is not that free. The traditional illustration of this phenomenon can be found in the Fox and the Grapes (cf. Izuma et al., 2010), which addresses the willingness and the wisdom of depreciating an inaccessible object of desire. This paradigm extends to difficult cases of renunciation, in which the decision is somewhat forced. The

---

[4] Shareholders are not free to choose the firm's production plan, but are free to decide whether or not they wish to remain shareholders.

'sour grapes preferences' described by Elster (1983) are of this kind, and can be invoked in support of the Pareto principle.

5.2.3 Is It Sensible to Change One's Preferences?

It is clear that if rationality is understood as a set of properties from the preference relation—completeness and transitivity, for example—then it is impossible to conceive of rational preference shifts. This would mean introducing the notion of metarationality and defining a preference relation over preferences.

Gilboa (2011) offers an attractive understanding of metarationality that is specific to the individual. Imagine an individual who makes choices that do not comply with a behavioral axiom considered to be a standard of rationality. His behavior is irrational with respect to this axiomatic definition, but is it irrational beyond that? Now let us imagine that we can talk to him, explain the behavioral axiom he has violated, and ask what he thinks. If he is embarrassed and swears to live by this axiom in the future, then yes, we can deem his initial choice irrational. If, on the contrary, he sees no problem in his behavior and says he is willing to repeat the same choice with full awareness of the violated axiom, then perhaps his choice was not so irrational after all.

This gives us every reason to see changes in preferences which are likely to improve individual welfare as far from irrational. When one is exposed to a source of harm that cannot be overcome, or which is too costly to neutralize, working on the self so as to become indifferent to it is a patent sign of wisdom. Our brain is a valuable ally in this respect, quickly learning not to smell or hear familiar unpleasant odors or noises.

This brings us back to the duality between preferences and goods. If optimization is a pillar of the economic approach, it is only natural in the context of a failed market and the impossibility of adjusting the quantities consumed to open up alternative spaces of freedom in which to optimize. It is easy to formally represent this opening using a cardinal approach to utility; if the problem

$$\arg\max\{u(x) \mid x \in X\}$$

is trivial because the set of choices $X = \{\bar{x}\}$ is a singleton, then individual welfare can only be improved by the possibility of a change in preferences: $u \in U$, which gives us the solution

$$\arg\max\{u(\bar{x}) \mid u \in U\}$$

(having neutralized affine transformations, of course). The notion of adaptive preference (Elster, 1983; Sen, 1985; von Weizsäcker, 2013) is of this ilk.[5]

5.3 The Ethics of Adaptation

To return to the fundamentals of the Pareto principle, we can see that there may be excellent reasons, if not a form of rationality in its own right, for adapting to the unanimous views of the groups with which we are affiliated, or even to adopt them outright. For everything points to the inevitability that they will be imposed and form a state of affairs common to all. For an individual, it seems perfectly reasonable to adapt to such inexorable circumstances.

Let us look back to the logic underpinning such reasoning when it comes to beliefs. If all of the firms in which an individual invests opt for a certain type of strategy based on a shared belief about the future states of the world, a belief with respect to which that individual is agnostic, then there are two possibilities: either he sells his investments and leaves these collective entities, or he freely decides to stay on, in which case he may as well embrace the future depicted and adhere to the unanimous vision presented. Can the same apply to tastes?

5.3.1 Autonomy

Elster (1983) reasons that a parallel can be established between beliefs and tastes by presenting the notion of autonomy as being to desires what judgments are to beliefs:[6]

> [...] autonomous desires are desires that have been deliberately chosen, acquired or modified—either by an act of will or by a process of character planning.

---

[5] It is used to explain how people living in abject misery manage to be satisfied with their lot. It is also why some economists express doubts about public policies developed based on the preferences of their beneficiaries and look to *capacities* rather than welfare to evaluate those policies (Sen, 1985, 1999; Nussbaum, 2003, 2004).

[6] Elster (1983) admits that he is unable to go beyond this analogy and provide a positive definition of autonomy (p. 128), but offers an ostensive definition: "Just as there are persons well known for their judgement, there are persons that are apparently in control over the processes whereby their desires are formed, or at least are not in the grip of processes with which they do not identify themselves" (p. 21).

For both desires and beliefs, one crucial condition of rationality is the absence of distortions or illusions. As has been emphasized, a collective judgment could be considered a less subjective belief, not to the extent that it is based on observable and opposable facts, but because it is less skewed by personal bias. And in this regard, councils and assemblies can be considered "persons well known for their judgment." They have their own rules, which in itself makes them autonomous in the etymological sense of the term. To paraphrase Elster, they control the processes through which their (implicit) beliefs and tastes are formed, or at least they are not in the grip of processes whereby individual tastes and beliefs are formed. If scoria of distortions and illusions were to remain at the aggregate level, they would be swept away in the reciprocal aggregation process by the multiple iterations of the Pareto principle. Last but not least, the absence of distortions or illusions is guaranteed by the reflexivity preserved by the Pareto principle at the individual level: it allows an indifference to expand into a preference, but does not suggest a reversal of preferences, a condition for autonomy of preferences, according to Elster (1983, p. 131).

According to Dworkin (1988, p. 20):

> Autonomy is conceived of as a second-order capacity of persons to reflect critically upon their first-order preferences, desires, wishes, and so forth and the capacity to accept or attempt to change these in light of higher-order preferences and values.

Here, too, the mechanism of individual aggregation S (see the introduction to Chapter 4) can be seen as a capacity for critical reflection about one's initial preferences; and the successive iterations of reciprocal aggregation create the conditions for higher-order in-depth critical reflection. Similarly, *affectio societatis* can be considered a higher-order value.

The notion of higher-order preferences can also be found in the work of Elster (1983), in the distinction between 'sour grapes' and 'character planning' preferences. In short, the former involve downgrading inaccessible objects of consumption, whereas the latter involve embellishing those that are accessible; the former come about as a result of temperament and are more endured than chosen, whereas the latter develop through reasoning and are deliberately chosen. In his attempt to distinguish between the two, Bovens (1992) describes character planning preferences as indicative of a better developed project in which preferences are adapted, as are the *reasons* for their adaptation.

5.3.2 Freedom and Conformity

'Making a virtue of necessity' is compatible with freedom. Paradoxically, some people believe that adapting one's preferences is a 'liberation strategy'. Is it not the case that the Stoic doctrine describes freedom as the strength and courage to embrace an inevitable future? Goldman (1972) wrote:

> The Stoics, and Spinoza as well, recommended that one forms one's desires to accord with what can realistically be expected to happen in any case; they regarded freedom as conformity of events with actual desires, or rather, as conformity of desires with events.   (p. 223)

This leaves us to understand at what point adapting one's tastes is about more than mere conformism or imitation, no matter how autonomous. The following quote from Simmel (1955) sweeps away the idea that through the aggregation mechanism $\mathcal{S}$ an individual sheds some of his profound identity:

> It is true that external and internal conflicts arise through the multiplicity of group-affiliations, which threaten the individual with psychological tensions or even a schizophrenic break. But it is also true that multiple group-affiliations can strengthen the individual and reenforce the integration of his personality. Conflicting and integrating tendencies are mutually reenforcing. Conflicting tendencies can arise just because the individual has a core of inner unity. The ego can become more clearly conscious of this unity, the more he is confronted with the task of reconciling within himself a diversity of group-interests. [. . .] These conflicts may induce the individual to make external adjustments, but also to assert himself energetically.   (pp. 141–142)

This is a view that is shared by philosophers of collective action, e.g. List & Pettit (2011):

> The picture drawn suggests that we form and enact not only beliefs and desires that mark each of us in our individuality but also those of various group agents we are associated with. These range from schools and universities to churches, from voluntary associations to activist groups, from town meetings to political parties and the states we live in. We may sometimes find it difficult to remain steadily committed to the group agents we are part of; our different commitments may clash. But generally our membership in group agents, active or aspirational, provides us with novel channels of identification and self-identification.
>
> (p. 195)

Beyond the traditional arguments of sociology or philosophy, three arguments in particular tear apart a critique of the Pareto principle (at the individual level) as sheer conformism. The first is linked to the difference in nature between the preferences of individuals and the judgments of groups: an individual does not take into consideration the preferences of other individuals, but rather those of the groups to which he belongs. The aim is not therefore to imitate one's peers. Nor is it about conformism in the passive sense of the term, but instead about actively conforming with the 'party line' which one has deliberately chosen rather than the norms and customs inherited through the circumstances of one's birth. Second, and to extend this metaphor, an individual can potentially be affiliated with a large number of parties and synthesize their respective lines; and it is not to be forgotten that the Pareto principle only implies a change in preferences when there is mass alignment in the form of unanimity among all the parties one has joined. Third, and most importantly, we insist that the Pareto principle at the individual level only imposes a strengthening—and not a reversal—of preferences.

Let us now attempt to axiomatize the preferences based on value vectors.

5.4 The Axiomatics of Adaptation

Given a production plan $\bar{y}$, with a little poetic license one can consider the firm to have an induced (linear) preference which it maximizes; this is defined on the boundary $\partial \mathcal{Y}$ of the production set by the following operator

$$\succeq_{\bar{y}}: y \to \nabla(\bar{y}) \cdot y$$

where $\nabla_j(\bar{y}) \in \mathbb{S}^\ell$ is the value vector at $\bar{y}$. The relation

$$\succeq_{\cdot}: y \to \succeq_{\bar{y}}$$

is an example of a preference that depends on a reference point (Kahneman & Tversky, 1979), which in this case is the chosen production plan, or the rational anticipation thereof. It is noteworthy that on $\partial \mathcal{Y}$, y is the best possible production plan for the induced preference $\succeq_y$:

$$\forall y, y' \in \partial \mathcal{Y}, \ y \succeq_y y'.$$

As a tribute to Nietzsche, we will call this property *amor fati*.

Definition 5.1 *A preference* $(\succeq.)$ *is **amor fati** over a set* P *if*

$$\forall a, b \in P, a \succeq_a b.$$

*A contrario it is **odium fati** if*

$$\forall a, b \in P, b \succeq_a a.$$

It is important to remember at this stage that *amor fati* type preferences are not purely conservative. They can be seen as dynamic: the reference point (in this case a) can be an anticipated point on which everyone coordinates.

At a reciprocal aggregation equilibrium $(p^\star, U^\star, \theta^\star, x^\star, y^\star)$, consumer i has the induced preference $(\succeq_{i,(U^\star, x^\star)})$ out of the set of production plans; this is defined by the value vector $\nabla_i(U^\star, x^\star)$. The following observation is an immediate corollary of the fact that within a cluster all value vectors are identical.

Proposition 5.1 *Let* $(p^\star, U^\star, \theta^\star, x^\star, y^\star)$ *be a reciprocal aggregation equilibrium. Then for every* i, j

$$\text{for all } y_j \in \partial \mathcal{Y}_j, y_j^\star \succeq_{i,(U^\star, x^\star)} y_j.$$

Our poetic license allows us to qualify preference $(\succeq_{i,\cdot})$ as *amor fati*. The diabolical example in Section 3.5 stands in stark contrast. If consumers anticipate that y_C will prevail in the future, then all (new) shareholders prefer y_B. So within the set of possibilities $\{y_C, y_B\}, y_B \succeq_{y_C} y_C$ for all shareholders. Their collective preference is *odium fati*.

5.4.1 Consistency and Rationalization

Can we go further than this ordinal consistency and make any assertion about cardinal consistency? In the presence of production externalities (Section 4.3), portfolio transactions are neutral in terms of wealth and have no impact on the level of utility, even if they modify the induced preferences. Similarly, in the context of an incomplete market (Section 4.4), updating beliefs in no way affects the level of utility. And so in both cases adaptations of *amor fati* type preferences are cardinally neutral.

We will not go into too much detail on the distinction between 'sour grapes' and 'character planning' preferences, between which lies a gray area. But the notion of *amor fati* preference probably applies more to the latter than the former if we follow the analysis of Bovens (1992), for whom character planning relates to a more developed project *since the reasons for adapting one's preferences are themselves adapted.* Portfolio transactions designed to ensure internal choice consistency (Section 4.3) or updated beliefs (Section 4.4) do precisely that.

5.4.2 Adaptive Preferences

Let us consider the notion of an adaptive preference out of a set of possibilities $\mathcal{P}$. It is based on the principle that for a given plan a, becoming the reference point only serves to strengthen preferences for a (positive adaptation) or exacerbate its rejection (negative adaptation).

Definition 5.2 *A preference* $(\succeq.)$ *is **positively adaptive** over a set* $\mathcal{P}$ *if* [7]

$$\forall a, b, c \in \mathcal{P}, a \succeq_c b \Rightarrow a \succeq_a b \text{ and } a \succ_c b \Rightarrow a \succ_a b.$$

*It is **negatively adaptive** if*

$$\forall a, b, c \in \mathcal{P}, b \succeq_c a \Rightarrow b \succeq_a a \text{ and } b \succ_c a \Rightarrow b \succ_a a.$$

A fixed preference $(\succeq)$—independent of all reference points—is trivially adaptive. In contrast, we can imagine that a preference $(\succeq.)$ out of a set of possibilities $\mathcal{P}$ would exhibit *complete flexibility* if the comparison between two alternatives were not absolute but always relative:

$$\forall a, b \in \mathcal{P}, \exists c \in \mathcal{P} \text{ such that } a \succeq_c b.$$

This immediately points to the following property.

Remark 5.1 *A positively adaptive and completely flexible preference is amor fati. A negatively adaptive and completely flexible preference is odium fati.*

---

[7] Von Weizsäcker (2013) offers a weaker definition: $\forall a, b \in \mathcal{P}, a \succeq_b b \Rightarrow a \succeq_a b$ and $a \succ_b b \Rightarrow a \succ_a b.$

5.5 Collective Agency and Social Responsibility

We have insisted that both our thesis of reciprocal aggregation and our hypothesis of a two-way Pareto principle (from individuals to collective and vice versa) are fully compatible with methodological individualism, i.e. the view that social phenomena only result from the agency of individuals. Yet when we talk about collective action, or judgment, it is not just a metaphor: group agents are real and count in their own right, independently of their members; through their organizations, processes, and decision protocols, they bring distinctive autonomous features that are extrinsic to their individual members and retroact at the individual level. In that sense our thesis lies within the *realist* approach to group agency, as opposed to the *eliminativist* approach[8] that, according to List & Pettit (2011), emerged and prevailed in the twentieth century among philosophers and social theorists.

5.5.1 A Realistic Realist Approach to Group Agency

Although realist, our thesis does not assume some psychologically mysterious force (Pettit, 1993). If there is a shared purpose, it is purely driven by material considerations and embedded in an organizational, procedural or legal framework. Assemblies of shareholders or stakeholders, even though real agents, are not "animated" in the sense that their agency "requires something above and beyond the emergence of coordinated, psychologically intelligible dispositions in individual members" (List & Pettit, 2011). The consideration that collective judgments respectful of the Pareto principle are averaging out individual biases, and in that sense are less subjective than individual beliefs, is as intelligible as Proposition 2.1 can be; the consideration that chosen group affiliation (here based on shared financial and insurance needs) as opposed to random group affiliation creates a special disposition of individuals toward groups' judgments is not mysterious; neither is making a virtue of necessity, especially material necessity.

Hence our thesis remains methodologically individualistic, and yet groups are not redundant: the mechanics of group decision-making shape individual beliefs and desires. This is very much in line with the theory of List & Pettit

---

[8] According to the eliminativist approach, there are only individual agents, and when they interact, coordinate or act together, they do not give rise to new agents; hence any group-agency talk is either metaphorical or misconceived.

(2011). For these authors, the non-redundancy of group agents comes from the fact that, having to satisfy certain minimal requirements of consistency, a group agent may be led to form judgments that depart from the beliefs of their members; to escape the multitude of impossibility theorems, it may even have to form a judgment on some issue that all its members individually reject—a negation of the Pareto principle. Our thesis sheds new light on the question: methodological individualism can account for non-redundant group agents who respect the Pareto principle if one applies this principle both ways.

5.5.2 From Agency to Responsibility

Real or not, corporations are by definition legal persons. Their personhood flows from their taking real actions that impact individual agents—a personhood that might be artificial, but is not fictional. And as a consequence corporations are ascribed *corporate responsibility*. Discussing the extent to which this corporate responsibility is a collective responsibility, of the shareholders or stakeholders, goes beyond the scope of this essay. But quite prosaically, boards of directors or general assemblies of shareholders make judgments and take decisions that have a normative content; they control the processes through which their judgments are formed and their decisions are taken; they have obligations toward other persons, first of all contractual obligations, and why not social obligations?

This leads us to the debate about corporate social responsibility, and what our thesis brings to it.

5.6 Individual Freedom and Social Responsibility

A founder of the so-called 'shareholder theory,' sometimes called the Friedman doctrine, Friedman (1962) asserts that "there is one and only one social responsibility of business—to use its resources and engage in activities designed to increase its profits so long as it stays within the rules of the game, which is to say, engages in open and free competition without deception or fraud." Later, in the *New York Times Magazine*, Friedman (1970) vilified corporate executives who go beyond this, e.g. those who would "refrain from increasing the price of their product in order to contribute to the social objective of preventing inflation," or those who would "make expenditures on reducing pollution beyond the amount that is in the best interests of the corporation or that is required by law in order to contribute to the social objective of improving the environment" (two examples well understood in our models of monopolistic behavior and production externalities). The main argument is that, in each of these cases, the corporate executive would be spending someone else's money for a general social interest, i.e. imposing a tax—a prerogative that he says should be left to elected public representatives. He concludes: "the use of the cloak of social responsibility [. . .] does clearly harm the foundations of a free society. [. . .] It would extend the scope of the political mechanism to every human activity."

5.6.1 No, the Social Responsibility of Business Is Not Necessarily to Increase Its Profits

We unearth this militant text to resume the conversation between our hardcore neoclassical economist and her more tempered colleague. Friedman is certainly a brilliant specimen of the former kind. We can only commend him for the clarity and logical rigor of his argument. But even if we adopt his restricted view of social responsibility, we must conclude that it is not necessarily profit maximization. If it is reasonable to expect a corporate executive to serve the interests of the firm's owners, it is doubtful that, in a publicly owned firm, these interests are aligned. Even purely materialist owners may not want to maximize profits (as in the case of externalities or imperfect competition), or may not agree on how to compute profits (as in the case of an incomplete market). GAs are meetings where attendees are not necessarily unanimous. Hence yes, the scope of the political mechanism has to be extended, at least to decision-making in the firm. And if the fruit of this political mechanism is economic efficiency, then a hard-core neoclassical economist should welcome it—and if that means giving equal voting rights to all stakeholders and imposing a stakeholder democracy as the rules of the game, the economist has no legitimacy to object, as this is a question of property rights allocation, a prerogative of the sovereign collective, most often the state.

If being honest, even our hard-core neoclassical economist would acknowledge the necessity of resorting to political mechanisms to resolve disputes between free individual agents on the market.[9] She would insist that these

---

[9] Friedman (1970, p. 17) himself does so, as he writes: "Unfortunately, unanimity is not always feasible. There are some respects in which conformity appears unavoidable, so I do not see how one can avoid the use of the political mechanism altogether."

disputes are residual, and would question their significance. She might even accept the possibility that assets be traded for internal choice consistency (as in Section 4.3 to internalize externalities), or the possibility of flexible preferences, especially the flexibility of beliefs (as in Section 4.4 in the context of an incomplete market). There is not much in all this that hurts the doctrine of free trade rationally exercised by individual agents.

5.6.2 Social Responsibility Is Compatible with Individual Freedom

So, if the social responsibility of business is not necessarily to increase its profits, what is it? According to Friedman (1970, p. 17): "There are no values, no 'social' responsibilities in any sense other than the shared values and responsibilities of individuals. Society is a collection of individuals and of the various groups they voluntarily form." Let us for a moment endorse this eliminativist view on collectives. At the end of the day, firms take decisions that are approved by the shareholders or stakeholders. If, for example, because they all hold the market portfolio, shareholders push for expenditure on reducing pollution beyond the amount that is in the best interests of the corporation (see Remark 3.1), what is the problem? And if they hold the market portfolio just for the sake of internal choice consistency (see Section 4.3), what is the problem? In that case the corporation serves all the interests of its shareholders, and only those interests.

More generally, if the individual interests of shareholders or stakeholders are to pursue social responsibility at the expense of profits, it is their privilege and prerogative to do so. This is nevertheless questioned by Friedman, who also vilifies those who call upon shareholders to require corporations to exercise social responsibility. At best, he would tolerate what he calls "hypocritical window-dressing": rationalize actions that are entirely justified by one's own self-interest as an exercise of social responsibility.[10] Making a virtue of necessity would be a more generous way to refer to such an attitude.

Suppose a socially responsible production plan emerges from majority voting, as Propositions 3.1 and 3.2 suggest, even though it does not exactly match the individual interest of any voter; what's wrong with that? Individual agents trade and vote freely and, icing on the cake, social responsibility

---

[10] For example, stockholders contributing more to charities they favor by having the corporation make the gift in their stead, given the laws about the deductibility of corporate charitable contributions, since that way they can contribute an amount that would otherwise have been paid as corporate taxes.

results in economic efficiency (maximizing joint profits by internalizing externalities in Proposition 3.1, and competitive pricing for the monopoly in Proposition 3.2)!

5.6.3 The Intrusion of Political Mechanisms onto the Market

At its core, what Friedman seems to dislike is not so much social responsibility as the intrusion of politics onto the market; as he writes: "The doctrine of 'social responsibility' involves the acceptance of the socialist view that political mechanisms, not market mechanisms, are the appropriate way to determine the allocation of scarce resources to alternative uses." The fear is that political mechanisms will press individual agents to conform to some collective views against their free will.

The opposition between the economics of resource allocation and the politics of social choice is based on principles. As Friedman puts it:

> The political principle that underlies the market mechanism is unanimity. In an ideal free market resting on private property, no individual can coerce any other, all cooperation is voluntary, all parties to such cooperation benefit or they need not participate. [. . .]
>
> The political principle that underlies the political mechanism is conformity. The individual must serve a more general social interest— whether that be determined by a church or a dictator or a majority. The individual may have a vote and say in what is to be done, but if he is overruled, he must conform. It is appropriate for some to require others to contribute to a general social purpose whether they wish to or not.
>
> (1970, p. 17)

This opposition is a bit schematic. Conformity is not absent from the market: behavioral economics has shown that individual agents conform to social norms—fairness, for example—and in Section 5.3 we argue that conformity is compatible with freedom. Inversely, unanimity is always present in the polity, as when people vote, they do so with a ballot and not with their feet: by construction all voters have unanimously chosen to stay within the polity, as opposed to defect and leave—the extent to which it is a free choice might also be debated, as it is not always easy to vote with one's feet (even less so as a citizen than as a resident of some jurisdiction), but it is easy in the present context: one need only sell one's shares.

This opposition on the basis of principles is not an opposition on the basis of functioning. Where the market mechanism fails, a political mechanism is necessary. The first part of this essay further argues that the less the market mechanism fails, the better the political mechanism works; and the political mechanism can help foster economic efficiency. The second part of this essay highlights the aggregation mechanism that takes place within the inner self of the individual; it shows conditions under which the joint operation of both aggregation mechanisms totally restores economic efficiency. It is noteworthy that the main condition is that both aggregation mechanisms, hence the political mechanism, respect the Pareto principle—a principle that imposes no action unless there is . . . unanimity.

5.6.4 Why There Is Hope

The thesis proposed in this essay shines a light of hope on collective agency. Even if we adopt the uncompromising view that individual agents are selfish, only motivated by their material interests and initially insensitive to any social responsibility,[11] the outcome of their interaction on the market and in the economic interest groups they form can be fully socially responsible. The indeterminacy of equilibrium highlighted in Remark 4.2 is very helpful here: not only is the outcome socially responsible in the core economic sense of efficiently allocating scarce resources, but it could endogenously conform to other virtues, made out of necessity, if there are shared expectations of the ineluctability of such outcomes.

Footnote 2 in Chapter 4 depicted the absurdity of self-fulfilling beliefs on financial markets, and showed why an accumulation of individual reasons does not necessarily lead to collective reason. This dark statement has its bright counterpart: an accumulation of individual unreasons does not necessarily lead to collective unreason. In the matter, every little helps.

---

[11] In their analysis of voting by institutional investors and public pensions funds on proxy ballots, Bolton et al. (2019, p. 4) find that "institutional investors' ideal points map onto a line, where the far-left investors are best described as socially responsible investors (those who vote most consistently in favor of pro-social and proenvironment shareholder proposals), and the far-right investors can be described as 'moneyconscious' investors (those who oppose proposals that could financially cost shareholders). In other words, the issue that most separates institutional investors is the degree to which they weigh social responsibility."

Conclusion

On the Road with Democracy and the Market

This last section summarizes the content of the book and provides some concluding comments.

Summary of the Book

The book explores how individuals and collectives interact, by trading and voting, on the market and in accordance with the democratic principle. Democracy and the market are two institutions that allow consumers to express their opinions on various issues. The fundamental subject of the book is how these two institutions work together to promote consensus and performance in economic and political life. The main finding is that they can mitigate some of each other's shortcomings.

The first part of the book focuses on how the market shapes the behavior of collectives through individual consumption and investment, and in turn how collectives shape the market through majority voting. It highlights how the interplay between trading and voting fosters political stability and economic efficiency. On the one hand, markets make consumers have identical marginal valuations of different commodities; thereby, consumers as voters become more aligned, making collective decisions easier to take, and less conservative. On the other hand, collectives of shareholders have broader interests than just individual firms; and the expression of these broader interests through majority voting can mitigate market failures.

The second part of the book dwells on another linkage between individuals and collectives, namely how collective decisions directly shape individuals' opinions. The main theme is the Pareto principle according to which consumers' opinions are modified so that they are not at odds with the decisions taken by the collectives in which the consumers take part, when all collectives agree. The Pareto principle has a remarkably strong implication: it leads to

Democracy, the Market, and the Firm: How the Interplay between Trading and Voting Fosters Political Stability and Economic Efficiency. Hervé Crès and Mich Tvede, Oxford University Press. © Hervé Crès and Mich Tvede 2021. DOI: 10.1093/oso/9780192894731.003.0007

complete alignment of opinions between economic agents. As a result, all shortcomings of the market and collective decision-making are eliminated.

The model presented in this book is minimalistic. It only has two types of agents: shareholders and GAs. It includes no intermediary: no banker, no director or board member, no regulator, and no media. This makes for a clearer and simpler message, and may help those who find the model too crude to identify those elements most lacking. It may be deficient in realism but is intended to account for the essential and avoids the trap of seeking to stick too close to reality and ultimately distorting rather than describing it. However, the model is postmodern in that the only hard realities are technologies. Beliefs and preferences can evolve through reciprocal aggregation without much consequence for consumers.

Reciprocal Aggregation and the Pareto Principle

The thesis of reciprocal aggregation may be original but it is no more than the concatenation of a traditional approach in economics (the aggregation of individual preferences to reach collective decisions) and a no less traditional approach in sociology (the formation of individual preferences through the influence of collective affiliations), both of which are perfectly compatible with a traditional notion used in political science (deliberation). This union between holism and methodological individualism may seem unnatural, and the fruit it bears—reciprocal aggregation—may appear as a chimera (in at least two meanings of the term: hybrid animal and fanciful conception), but it is a chimera that produces undeniably compelling results (the single thought theorem in particular) from notoriously weak hypotheses (the Pareto principle). There are doubtless other mechanisms that can explain the level of consensus observed at the GAs of firms listed on the CAC 40, and they too will doubtless have their detractors, beginning with the zealots of the perfect market thesis. Such is the nobility of academic debate, and if there is one debate that must be protected from single thought, it is that one.

The hypotheses underpinning the model are for the most part well established, with the exception of the Pareto principle being applied to individual decisions. For those who find this hypothesis unrealistic, a normative reading of Theorem 4.1 can be recommended. If we consider it desirable to have alignment between agents on the basis that it allows groups to move forward with the strength of unity and achieve their destinies, we should work towards the emergence of standards that direct individuals to respect the Pareto principle and rally behind the opinions of the groups to which they belong when all these groups agree. If we consider such consensus undesirable on the basis that it is too self-referential, converges haphazardly, and remains too exposed to the risk of manipulation, then we should encourage all individuals to maintain a certain reserve at all times and never to be intimidated by ambient single thought, even when it emanates from established authorities in the form of collective judgments.

Virtues and Vices of Consensus

This kind of consensus may be desirable in some contexts and undesirable in others. In strictly economic terms, if it does not involve any personal drama (for example, a layoff plan in a rigid labor market), then the alignment of shareholders can seem harmless. After all, we are simply talking about equalizing the marginal utility ratios of various goods and services consumed at various times and in various places; indeed, in some cases we are only talking about aligning beliefs about the probabilities that various economic scenarios will occur in the future, scenarios that are largely endogenous and with all kinds of prophecies about the likelihood of their occurrence, some of which are fulfilled simply because they were proffered and managed to convince a sufficient number of people. In sum, it is only a matter of aligning material values, not moral, and certainly not spiritual. Under no circumstances are we talking about brainwashing or forcing any kind of emotional or cognitive overhaul. It is true that the process of reciprocal aggregation converges towards a random value vector, but this matters little: in the absence of objective criteria with which to compare the many possible outcomes, they are all of equal value. Ultimately, it would appear that the alignment of shareholders, so indispensable for legitimacy and unified action, comes at a relatively modest price. And in a totally interconnected economy, the restoration of the first welfare theorem despite market failures (Corollary 4.2) is remarkable, even though the theorem has lost some of its splendor due to the malleability of individual preferences.

If we subscribe to the view that firms have many different possible paths to growth and that it matters little which one is chosen since the reality is that strength comes from unity and a firm's success is driven by mutual trust and dynamism, then the greatest possible number of individuals should be linked to the shareholder network. All policies that help broaden this network are a step in the right direction, beginning with incentives for employee shareholdings.[1] The sale of shares to stakeholders and all other measures to encourage their participation in the governance of firms are to be welcomed.

Of course there is a limit to the virtues of unanimity, even in economic matters. The effective (if not objective) probabilities that future economic scenarios will come about may be endogenous insofar as they depend on the beliefs and choices of the agents concerned, but this does not make them boundless: they are subject to physical constraints and factors that are extrinsic to economic activity, and we can safely say they are ultimately the result of the interplay between different forces, without lapsing into a deterministic point of view. And when the single thought feeds off beliefs that have drifted beyond all reason, brutal adjustments are to be expected, as in the case of the sub-prime collapse in 2007. The same can probably be said about marginal utility ratios. There's no accounting for taste, the saying goes. So it should matter little when the single thought feeds off eccentric revisions of personal tastes. However, this is only true up to a point: it is difficult to accept any single thought that is based on the acceptance by some of objectively miserable living conditions.

Beyond the Firm

Beyond strictly economic matters, there are fewer reasons to consider the emergence of single thought a desirable thing. First of all, the danger of brutal adjustments is to be feared just as much as in the economic context. The rejection of the 'system' that has become so popular in political debate in the West is also the rejection of single thought, that of the orthodox members of society who are perceived as having the privilege—or the good fortune—to hold orthodox views because the established order suits them. But when the orthodoxy, or correctness, of those who are connected strays too far from the realities people are facing, or rather from people's perception of these realities, then an election can suffice to bring about a shift, one that it is 'correct' to describe as populism. The 2016 elections in the United Kingdom and the United States are illustrations of this.

As well as the fear of brutal adjustments, one can only feel uneasy when faced with the alignment of values beyond the material world, in the moral or

---

[1] In France, the percentage of households with shareholdings increased from 13.9 to 23.1 percent between 1991 and 1998, according to the Observatoire de l'Epargne Européenne. In 1998, this figure reached 48.9 percent in the United States and 34.8 percent in the United Kingdom.

political sphere. First of all because it stinks of indoctrination. Not indoctrination by coercion or subjugation, but by connections and suggestion. There is no need for an authority to dictate a system of values and indoctrinate in schools or in camps; all that is needed is for each individual to have the weakness (or strength, depending on how you see it) to succumb to the unanimity of collective judgments in a connected society. The mechanisms are radically different but the outcome is the same. Of course, one might object that while there is alignment of values in both cases, reciprocal aggregation ensures that they pass through the filter of the judgments of many different groups and people, thereby promoting more ecumenical values. To rely on such hope would be to play a risky game: history provides many examples that counter the perceived wisdom of the crowd. But this essay will not be lost as a footnote on the comparative merits of moral and political values. If it is to contribute in any way to the debate, it is by warning of the consequences of systematically rallying behind the unanimous views of established groups (parties, firms, media, etc.); and that should apply to all views, even the most ecumenical.

For a Democracy of Stakeholders

So why not challenge the absolute reverence, in the West at least, for the democratic model as we know it? Sections 3.2 and 3.3 provide us with an illustration of the problem. If we are convinced that the democracy of stakeholders is superior to the oligarchy of shareholders, then this principle must be applied to the decisions of today's democratic governments. The question of externalities is the most thorny. The governments of our great democratic nations make decisions which have an impact on the welfare of the world's population as a whole. Yet only their national citizens get to have their say. There is every reason to believe that these decisions are far from optimal from the point of view of the human species (not to mention other species). The world's modern democracies offer limited benefits because of their limited hold over space.

Then there are limits over time, with the painful issue of inter-generational transfers. The first example that comes to mind is public debt in many Western countries, amassed over forty years by generations of baby boomers, which have soared with COVID-19 and now often exceed GDP. The development of nuclear energy is another example that offers an even more breathtaking perspective: it represents an investment whose benefits are enjoyed exclusively by current generations but whose cost (decontamination and treatment of radioactive waste) spans hundreds of thousands of years.

Our democracies are limited, just as markets are. Consider the limits in space: for example, it is striking to see how impactful the decisions of the US government are on the world economy; yet 96 percent of the world population is excluded from the democratic process that leads to it. It may seem naive to write it, but this can be compared to the exclusion of some consumers from some markets. Equally, one could deplore the absence of economic instruments that would entice the American people to internalize the externalities generated by their democratic choices; or deplore the 'monopolistic' power of the American people over the world's economy.

As for limits in time, if one holds up the ideal of stakeholder democracy, then every decision with an impact on the welfare of future generations should be subject to a vote by those same people. But there is no mechanism, no 'venerable assembly' or 'council of sages,' in our modern democracies that can defend their point of view: similar to an incomplete market, there is no democratic instrument that allows future generations to weigh on today's collective choices that will impact so heavily their welfare. This runs the risk of relativizing the primacy of democracy (in the form that we know it) within the value scale that applies to the different forms of popular government. Our Western democracies should not install the tyranny of today's humans—the soon-to-be-dead—over those who have yet to be born.

What democracy and the market accomplish, in separate ways, is well understood; so are their shortcomings. In the first part of the book, we have highlighted what else they accomplish together, by mitigating each other's shortcomings. This could strengthen our faith in democracy and the market; yet we should make sure that this faith does not doom us. The residual shortcomings are worrisome. Even if they can apparently vanish through such mechanisms as reciprocal aggregation, as we have shown in the second part of the book, the resulting political consensus and economic efficiency can be so distant from reality that drastic, potentially catastrophic adjustments are ineluctable. Indeed, quoting H.G. Wells: "Civilization is in a race between education and catastrophe."

Votes in GAs—CAC 40, 2011–15

Companies listed on the CAC40 hold a GA annually, attended on average by around a thousand shareholders. Over the period 2011–15, a total of 3861 proposals were submitted to a vote by shareholders at GAs. A small number (29) were submitted without the consent of the board, or were alternatives to other proposals, and were subsequently voted down by a very large majority. They are withdrawn from the dataset, even though they would have only marginally affected the findings.

These decisions can be split into three categories: 1) *Collective* decisions, such as the approval of the company's financial statements, the setting of dividends, the delegation of authority to the board members, amendments to the company's charter etc.; 2) Decisions on *individual* compensation of senior managers and board members; 3) Decisions on the *appointment* or renewal of individual board members.

The following table shows, for each category, the total number of decisions and, as percentages, the lowest, highest and average support for all considered decisions, and the consensus index.

Decisions/Score	Number	Min. %	Max. %	Avg. %	Index %
Collective	2746	14.8	100	94.8	87.1
Individual	268	53.2	99.9	88.8	78
Appointment	818	9.2	100	83.7	86.4
Total	3832	9.2	100	94.2	86.3

This table can be broken down per year. In 2015, out of 822 propositions submitted to a vote, 817 were adopted.

Decisions/Score	Number	Min. %	Max. %	Avg. %	Index %
Collective	570	17.5	99.9	94	87.2
Individual	96	53.2	99.9	87.2	77.5
Appointment	151	59.6	99.9	95.1	87.5
Total	817	17.5	99.9	93.4	84.3

In 2014, out of 800 propositions submitted to a vote, 793 were adopted.

Decisions/Score	Number	Min. %	Max. %	Avg. %	Index %
Collective	519	17.1	100	96.2	89.4
Individual	99	53.7	99.7	89.2	78.8
Appointment	175	50.3	100	94.3	87.5
Total	793	17.1	100	94.9	87.6

In 2013, out of 746 propositions submitted to a vote, 739 were adopted.

Decisions/Score	Number	Min. %	Max. %	Avg. %	Index %
Collective	548	22.6	100	95.2	87.5
Individual	32	54.7	99.8	91.8	85.1
Appointment	159	20.8	100	93.4	87
Total	**739**	**20.8**	**99.9**	**94.7**	**87**

In 2012, out of 708 propositions submitted to a vote, 699 were adopted.

Decisions/Score	Number	Min. %	Max. %	Avg. %	Index %
Collective	514	14.8	100	94.4	87
Individual	17	61.8	99.6	86.5	75
Appointment	168	9.2	99.9	92.7	86
Total	**699**	**9.2**	**100**	**93.6**	**86.4**

In 2011, out of 785 propositions submitted to a vote, 784 were adopted.

Decisions/Score	Number	Min. %	Max. %	Avg. %	Index %
Collective	595	28.8	100	94.3	85.8
Individual	24	66.6	99.7	90.7	80
Appointment	165	60.9	99.9	93.1	84.3
Total	**784**	**28.8**	**100**	**93.6**	**85.5**

APPENDIX B

Proofs of the Results

Proof Lemma 1.1

(i) There is y_j such that $g_j(y_j) < 0$ because g_j is strictly convex. There is y'_j such that $g_j(y'_j) > 0$ because $\mathcal{Y}_j$ is compact and $\mathcal{Y}_j = \{ y_j \mid g_j(y_j) \leq 0 \}$. Therefore there is y''_j such that $g_j(y''_j) = 0$. For all y_j and y'_j, $g_j(y'_j) \geq g_j(y_j) + Dg_j(y_j) \cdot (y'_j - y_j)$ because g is convex. Assume $g_j(y_j) = 0$ and $g_j(y'_j) < 0$, then $Dg_j(y_j) \cdot (y'_j - y_j) < 0$, so $Dg_j(y_j) \neq 0$. Hence $g_j(y_j) = 0$ implies $y_j \in \partial Y_j$. Clearly $g_j(y_j) \neq 0$ implies $y_j \notin \partial \mathcal{Y}_j$.

(ii) Suppose $y_j \in \partial \mathcal{Y}_j$ and $Dg_j(y_j)$ and ∇_j are collinear. For all y'_j with $g_j(y'_j) \leq 0$ and $y'_j \neq y_j$, $Dg_j(y_j) \cdot (y'_j - y_j) < 0$ because g_j is strictly convex. Therefore y_j is optimal with respect to ∇. Suppose $y_j \in \mathcal{Y}_j$ with $y_j \notin \partial \mathcal{Y}_j$. Then $g_j(y'_j) < 0$ so there is $\varepsilon > 0$ such that $g_j(y_j + \varepsilon \nabla_j) \leq 0$. Hence y_j is not optimal with respect to ∇_j. Suppose $Dg_j(y_j)$ and ∇_j are not collinear. Then there is $v \in \mathbb{R}^S$ such that $Dg_j(y_j) \cdot v < 0 < \nabla_j \cdot v$ so there is $\varepsilon > 0$ such that $g_j(y_j + \varepsilon v) \leq 0$. Hence y_j is not optimal with respect to ∇_j.

(iii) It follows from the proof of (ii) that $y_j \in \partial \mathcal{Y}_j$ is optimal with respect to $Dg_j(y_j)$ and not with respect to any ∇_j that is not collinear with $Dg_j(y_j)$.

(iv) For all $\nabla_j \in \mathbb{R}^\ell \setminus \{0\}$ there is y_j such that y_j is optimal with respect to ∇_j because $\mathcal{Y}_j$ is compact. Suppose y_j and y'_j are both optimal with respect to ∇_j, then $g_j((1-\tau)y_j + \tau y'_j) < 0$ for all $\tau \in]0, 1[$ because g_j is strictly convex. Therefore for all $\tau \in]0, 1[$ there is $\varepsilon > 0$ such that $g_j((1-\tau)y_j + \tau y'_j + \varepsilon \nabla_j) \leq 0$. However $\nabla_j \cdot ((1-\tau)y_j + \tau y'_j + \varepsilon \nabla_j) > \nabla_j \cdot y_j = \nabla_j \cdot y'_j$ thus contradicting that y_j and y'_j are optimal with respect to $\nabla_j . \Diamond$

Proof of Lemma 1.2 The first-order conditions of the individual optimization problem for consumer i gives: $\exists \lambda_i \in \mathbb{R}_+$ such that $Du_i(x_i) = \Pi(\gamma_i 1_\ell - x_i) = \lambda_i p$. Hence $x_i = \gamma_i 1_\ell - \lambda_i \Pi^{-1} p$.

Denote $\Lambda = \sum_i \lambda_i$. Adding up the individual consumptions gives us: $\sum_i x_i = \Gamma 1_\ell - \Lambda \Pi^{-1} p = \Omega$, hence:

$$ p = \frac{1}{\Lambda} \Pi(\Gamma 1_\ell - \Omega) \text{ and } x_i = \gamma_i 1_\ell - \frac{\lambda_i}{\Lambda}(\Gamma 1_\ell - \Omega). $$

The price vector p is normalized, so that $p \cdot 1_\ell = 1$. As a consequence $\Lambda = \Gamma - \pi \cdot \Omega$. Hence the expression of p.

Denote $\alpha_i = \lambda_i / \Lambda$, hence the expression of x_i.

The equilibrium values of $(\alpha_i)_{i \in \mathcal{I}} \in \mathbb{S}_+^I$ are determined by the budget equations. Denote $\check{z}_i = \gamma_i 1_\ell - (\bar{x}_i + Y\bar{\theta}_i)$ the ideal transaction of i and $\check{z} = \sum_i \check{z}_i = \Gamma 1_\ell - \Omega$ the ideal aggregate. Since $x_i = \gamma_i 1_\ell - \alpha_i \check{z}$, one gets $p \cdot x_i = \gamma_i - \alpha_i p \cdot \check{z}$ (given the normalization of p). The latter equation associated with the budget equation $p \cdot x_i = p \cdot (\bar{x}_i + Y\bar{\theta}_i)$ yields

$$ \text{for every } i, \ \alpha_i = \frac{1}{p \cdot \check{z}}(\gamma_i - p \cdot (\bar{x}_i + Y\bar{\theta}_i)) \text{ with } p = \frac{1}{\pi \cdot \check{z}} \Pi \check{z}. $$

Since $\gamma_i - p \cdot (\bar{x}_i + Y\bar{\theta}_i) = p \cdot (\gamma_i 1_\ell - (\bar{x}_i + Y\bar{\theta}_i)) = p \cdot \check{z}_i$, simple transformations yield

$$\alpha_i = \frac{p \cdot \check{z}_i}{p \cdot \check{z}} = \frac{\check{z} \times_\pi \check{z}_i}{\|\check{z}\|_\pi^2} \text{ for every } i,$$

recalling the notation $y \times_\pi z = \sum_s \pi^s y^s z^s$. $\Diamond$

Proof of Lemma 1.3 (To lighten the notation, the indices i and j will be dropped, and ∇ stand for $\nabla_i^\|(x)$.) U is strictly quasi-concave, hence for all $x' \neq x$,

$$U(x') \geq U(x) \Rightarrow \nabla \cdot (x' - x) > 0.$$

Indeed, suppose $U(x') \geq U(x)$ and $\nabla \cdot (x' - x) \leq 0$. Then $U(x'') > U(x)$ for $x'' = (1 - a)x + ax'$ and all $a \in]0, 1[$ because U is strictly quasi-concave. Obviously $\nabla \cdot (x'' - x) \leq 0$. There is x''' (in all neighborhoods of x'') such that $U(x''') > U(x)$ and $\nabla \cdot (x''' - x) < 0$ because U is continuous. Since $\nabla \cdot (x''' - x) < 0$, there is $a \in]0, 1]$ such that $U((1 - a)x + ax''') < U(x)$ contradicting U is strictly quasi-concave. Hence, $U(x') > U(x)$ implies $\nabla \cdot (x' - x) > 0$. The first assertion follows directly given that $x' = x + \theta\Delta y$.

The reciprocal assertion is due to the strict quasi-concavity of U; Fig. B.1 helps understand why:

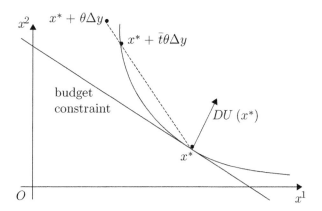

Fig. B.1 Minimum differentiation principle

For a large initial deviation Δy, it can be that despite $DU(x^*) \cdot \Delta y > 0$ one has: $U(x^* + \theta\Delta y) < U(x^*)$; by scaling down the deviation, there exists a threshold $\bar{t}$ for which $U(x^* + \bar{t}\theta\Delta y) = U(x^*)$, hence the desired property. $\Diamond$

Proof of Lemma 1.4 The first-order conditions of consumer i's optimization program give: $\exists \lambda_i \in \mathbb{R}_+$ such that $Y^T DU_i(x_i) = \lambda_i q \cdot i$. $\Diamond$

Proof of Lemma 1.5 Let us prove first that $\tilde{B}_i \subset B_i$. Take $x_i \in \tilde{B}_i$, then $x_i = \bar{x}_i + Y\theta_i$; hence $\nabla \cdot x_i = \nabla \cdot \bar{x}_i + \nabla \cdot Y\theta_i$. Note that $\nabla \cdot Y\theta_i = Y^T \nabla \cdot \theta_i = q \cdot \theta_i$.

Since $q \cdot \theta_i \leq q \cdot \bar{\theta}_i$, one has: $\nabla \cdot x_i \leq \nabla \cdot \bar{x}_i + q \cdot \bar{\theta}_i = \nabla \cdot \bar{x}_i + \nabla \cdot Y\bar{\theta}_i$, hence $x_i \in B_i$.

Inversely, let us prove that $B_i \subset \tilde{B}_i$. Take $x_i \in B_i$. Since markets are complete, there exists $\theta_i \in \mathbb{R}^J$ such that $x_i - \bar{x}_i = Y\theta_i$.

Let us check that $q \cdot \theta_i \leq q \cdot \bar{\theta}_i$. Since $x_i \in B_i$ one has $\nabla \cdot (x_i - \bar{x}_i) \leq \nabla \cdot Y\bar{\theta}_i$ hence $\nabla \cdot Y\theta_i \leq \nabla \cdot Y\bar{\theta}_i$, which is the inequality sought given that $\nabla \cdot Y\theta_i = q \cdot \theta_i$. $\Diamond$

Proof of Proposition 1.1 See Theorem 11.6 in Magill & Quinzii (1996).◇

Proof of Lemma 1.6 The necessary first-order conditions for the optimal choice of portfolio (cf. Lemma 1.4) give, for every i:

$$\lambda_i q = Y^T \Pi \left(\gamma_i 1_\ell - \bar{x}_i - Y \theta_i \right).$$

At equilibrium, adding up the preceding equations yields:

$$\Lambda q = Y^T \Pi \left(\Gamma 1_\ell - \Omega \right).$$

Given $\lambda_i q = Y^T \Pi \left(\gamma_i 1_\ell - \bar{x}_i \right) - \left(Y^T \Pi Y \right) \theta_i$ and the matrix $Y^T \Pi Y$ being invertible, replacing q by its equilibrium value one gets:

$$\theta_i = \left(Y^T \Pi Y \right)^{-1} Y^T \Pi \left[(\gamma_i - \alpha_i \Gamma) \, 1_\ell - (\bar{x}_i - \alpha_i \Omega) \right], \tag{B.1}$$

where $\alpha_i = \lambda_i / \Lambda$. Hence the result with $P_{\langle Y \rangle} = Y \left(Y^T \Pi Y \right)^{-1} Y^T \Pi$.

The equilibrium value of α_i is given by the budget condition $q \cdot \theta_i = q \cdot \bar{\theta}_i$ and takes the same value as in Lemma 1.2.

Recall that there exists a unique $\nabla \in \mathbb{S}_+^\ell$ such that $Y^T \nabla = q$, which implicitly normalizes q. This gives $\Lambda = \Gamma - \pi \cdot \Omega$ as in Lemma 1.2. As a result:

$$q = \frac{1}{\Gamma - \pi \cdot \Omega} Y^T \Pi \left(\Gamma 1_\ell - \Omega \right).$$

The interpretation for this is intuitive and well established: it is that of the CAPM. Assume that the first asset is without risk: $y_1 = 1_\ell$. The equilibrium price is therefore $q_1 = 1$. Denote $E_\pi(\Omega) = \pi \cdot \Omega$ the expected return of Ω. Then the formula for setting the price of asset j is:

$$q_j = E_\pi(y_j) - \frac{\text{cov}(\Omega, y_j)}{\Gamma - E_\pi(\Omega)}.$$

The value of an asset is the present value of its average return, y_j, added to which is a measure of the risk linked to its covariance with the aggregate shock in the economy, Ω.

A more common version of this model accounts for consumption at date 0, with linear quadratic utility functions:

$$U_i(x_i) = x_{i0} + \sum_{s=1}^{\ell} \pi^s \left(\gamma_i x_i^s - \frac{1}{2} (x_i^s)^2 \right) \tag{B.2}$$

Then the expression computed above remains valid for consumption in date 1, with $\alpha_i = 1/I$, independently of the production at date 0, which can therefore be discarded from the analysis. Hence, discarding date 0 coordinates, we get:

$$x_i^* = \bar{x}_i + \left(\gamma_i - \frac{\Gamma}{I} \right) P_{\langle Y \rangle} 1_\ell - P_{\langle Y \rangle} \left(\bar{x}_i - \frac{1}{I} \Omega \right).$$

In the context of Section 3.4, where $\gamma_i = \Gamma / I$ for all i, $\sum_i \bar{x}_i = 0$, states are equiprobable, and there is only one firm producing y such that $\|y\|^2 = I$, we get $P_{\langle Y \rangle} = \frac{1}{I} y y^T$ and

$$x_i^* = \bar{x}_i - \frac{1}{I} yy^T \left(\bar{x}_i - \frac{1}{I} y \right) = \bar{x}_i + \frac{1}{I}(1 - \bar{x}_i \cdot y)y.$$

$\diamond$

Proof of Lemma 1.7 Define the real function $H(t) = p \cdot Y(a_j(t), a_{-j})\bar{\theta}_i$. Thanks to the concavity of f_j, and given prices are positive, H is concave.

Let us prove the first assertion of the proposition. The left-hand side of the implication reads: $H(1) > H(0)$; and the right-hand side reads: $H'(0) > 0$. Obviously, by concavity of H, $H(1) > H(0) \Rightarrow H'(0) > 0$.

Reciprocally, if $H'(0) > 0$, then by continuity there exists $\bar{t} \in]0,1]$ such that $H(t) > H(0)$ for all $t \in]0, \bar{t}[$ which proves the second assertion of the proposition.$\diamond$

Proof of Proposition 1.2 (The subscript i, as well as the points at which functions are considered, are abandoned for lightness of the notation.) The consumer is better off with a marginal change Δy if and only if the consecutive change of utility level

$$\Delta u(h(p^*, w)) = Du^T (D_p h \, \Delta p + D_w h \, \Delta w)$$

is positive.

The first-order conditions of the consumer's optimization program mean that, at equilibrium, there exists $\lambda^* > 0$ such that $Du^T = \lambda^* p^{*T}$; hence $\Delta u(h(p, w)) > 0$ if and only if $p^{*T}(D_p h \, \Delta p + D_w h \, \Delta w) > 0$.

Walras' law: $p^{*T} h(p^*, w) = w$ implies $p^{*T} D_w h = 1$ and $p^{*T} D_p h = -h^T$. Therefore, the former conditions become: $-h^T \Delta p + \Delta w > 0$.

The results are obtained by replacing $\Delta w = (\bar{x} + Y\bar{\theta})^T \Delta p + \bar{\theta} p^T \Delta y$, $\Delta p = \Phi^T \Delta y$ and $h^T = x^{*T}$.$\diamond$

Proof of Proposition 2.1 According to Theorem 22.2 in Rockafellar (1970) either (where ∇_j does not respect the Pareto principle) there is $\Delta y \in \mathbb{R}^\ell$ such that

$$\nabla_i \cdot \Delta y \geq 0 \text{ for every } i \in I_j$$
$$\sum_{i \in I_j} \nabla_i \cdot \Delta y > 0$$
$$\nabla_j \cdot \Delta y \leq 0$$

or (where ∇_j does respect the Pareto principle) there are $(\alpha_i)_{i \in I_j}$ with $\alpha_i \geq 0$ for every i, $\beta > 0$ and $\gamma \geq 0$ such that

$$\sum_{i \in I_j} \alpha_i \nabla_i + \beta \sum_{i \in I_j} \nabla_i - \gamma \nabla_j = 0.$$

Clearly: $\alpha_i \geq 0$, $\nabla_i \in \mathbb{R}^\ell_{++}$ for every i and $\beta > 0$ imply $\gamma > 0$. Therefore

$$\nabla_j = \sum_{i \in I_j} \frac{\alpha_i + \beta}{\gamma} \nabla_i$$

hence the result.$\diamond$

Proof of Proposition 2.2 The proof of necessity goes by the contrapposed. Suppose ∇_j is not collinear to $\sum_{i \in \mathcal{I}_j} \nabla_i$. Then there exists $\Delta y \in \mathbb{R}^\ell$ such that $W = \sum_{i \in \mathcal{I}_j} \nabla_i \cdot \Delta y > 0$, and $\nabla_j \cdot \Delta y \leq 0$. Define the transfers

$$w_i = \frac{W}{|\mathcal{I}_j|} - \nabla_i \cdot \Delta y \text{ for every } i \in \mathcal{I}_j$$

Clearly, $\sum_{i \in \mathcal{I}_j} w_i = 0$, hence transfers $(w_i)_{i \in \mathcal{I}_j}$ are feasible. Moreover, $\nabla_i \cdot \Delta y + w_i > 0$ for every $i \in \mathcal{I}_j$. But $\nabla_j \cdot \Delta y \leq 0$. Hence ∇_j does not respect the Pareto principle with transfers.

The 'if' is immediate by contradiction. Suppose (without loss of generality) $\nabla_j = \sum_{i \in \mathcal{I}_j} \nabla_i$ does not respect the Pareto principle with transfers: $\exists \Delta y \in \mathbb{R}^\ell$ and feasible transfers $(w_i)_{i \in \mathcal{I}_j}$ such that $\nabla_i \cdot \Delta y + w_i \geq 0$ for every $i \in \mathcal{I}_j$ with $>$ for some $i \in \mathcal{I}_j$ and $-\nabla_j \cdot \Delta y \geq 0$. Adding all these inequalities, together with $\sum_{i \in M} w_i \leq 0$, yields $(-\nabla_j + \sum_{i \in \mathcal{I}_j} \nabla_i) \cdot \Delta y > 0$, in contradiction with $\nabla_j = \sum_{i \in \mathcal{I}_j} \nabla_i .\Diamond$

Proof of Lemma 2.1 If plan y_j is not stable, there exists $y'_j \in \mathcal{Y}_j$ such that $\nabla_i \cdot y'_j \geq \nabla_i \cdot y_j$ for every i with at least one strict inequality. Defining $\Delta y = y'_j - y_j$, one gets $\nabla_j(y_j) \cdot \Delta y \leq 0$ thanks to the convexity of $\mathcal{Y}_j$, and $\nabla_i \cdot \Delta y \geq 0$ for every i with at least one strict inequality. Therefore $\nabla_j(y_j)$ does not respect the Pareto principle.$\Diamond$

Proof of Proposition 2.4 (For lightness of notation, the subscript j is dropped.) For a deviation Δ, define the set of consumers whose value vector projects (orthogonally) onto T_y (the tangent space to $\partial \mathcal{Y}$ at y) along the line $\langle \Delta \rangle$:

$$\mathcal{M}(\Delta) = \left\{ i \mid \text{proj}_{T_y} \nabla_i = \beta \Delta, \text{ for some } \beta \in \mathbb{R} \right\}$$

Note that for all $\Delta, \mathcal{M}(0) \subset \mathcal{M}(\Delta)$. A consumer $i \in \mathcal{M}(0)$ if and only if $\nabla_i \in T_y^\perp$ which means that y is optimal for agent i. Hence the proposition holds if we prove $\mathcal{M}(0) \neq \emptyset$.

This follows from the following lemma.

Lemma B.1 *(Plott, 1967) The plan y is 0.5^- –stable within electorate $\mathcal{M}(\Delta)$.*

Indeed, a deviation Δ or $-\Delta$ will obtain at least half of the votes within electorate $\mathcal{M}(\Delta)$ (contradicting the above lemma) unless $\mathcal{M}(0) \neq \emptyset.\Diamond$

Proof of Lemma B.1 The proof goes by contradiction. For every group $\mathcal{M} \subset \mathcal{I}$, let $\lambda_j(\mathcal{M}) = \sum_{i \in \mathcal{M}} \lambda_i$ be the aggregate voting weight of group $\mathcal{M}$.

Suppose that a deviation $\bar{\Delta}$ wins in electorate $\mathcal{M}(\Delta)$; this means that the voting weight of $\bar{\mathcal{M}}(\Delta) \equiv \mathcal{I}(\bar{\Delta}) \cap \mathcal{M}(\Delta)$ (where $\mathcal{I}(\bar{\Delta})$ is the set of voters in favor of deviation $\bar{\Delta}$) contains at least half of the voting weight in $\mathcal{M}(\Delta)$:

$$2\lambda(\bar{\mathcal{M}}(\Delta)) \geq \lambda(\mathcal{M}(\Delta)). \tag{B.3}$$

Consider $\Delta' \in T_y \partial Y$ such that $\Delta' \perp \Delta$ and $\Delta' \perp \nabla_i \iff i \in \mathcal{M}(\Delta)$; such a Δ' exists given the finite number of consumers. The set of consumers is then partitioned into

$\mathcal{I}(\Delta') \cup \mathcal{I}(-\Delta') \cup \mathcal{M}(\Delta)$ whose voting weights sum up to 1:

$$\lambda(\mathcal{I}(\Delta')) + \lambda(\mathcal{I}(-\Delta')) + \lambda(\mathcal{M}(\Delta)) = 1. \tag{B.4}$$

Next, let $\Delta_1 = -\Delta' + \epsilon_1 \bar{\Delta}$ and $\Delta_2 = \Delta' + \epsilon_2 \bar{\Delta}$. For ϵ_1 and ϵ_2 that are small enough, one has the partition: $\mathcal{I}(\Delta_1) = \mathcal{I}(-\Delta') \cup \bar{\mathcal{M}}(\Delta)$ and $\mathcal{I}(\Delta_2) = \mathcal{I}(\Delta') \cup \bar{\mathcal{M}}(\Delta)$. Since y is 0.5^-−majority stable, these groups must be minorities:

$$
\begin{aligned}
0.5 &> \lambda(\mathcal{I}(-\Delta')) + \lambda(\bar{\mathcal{M}}(\Delta)) \\
0.5 &> \lambda(\mathcal{I}(\Delta')) + \lambda(\bar{\mathcal{M}}(\Delta))
\end{aligned}
$$

Adding them up together with inequalities (B.3) and (B.4) yields:

$$
\begin{aligned}
1 > \; & \lambda(\mathcal{I}(\Delta')) + \lambda(\mathcal{I}(-\Delta')) + 2\lambda(\bar{\mathcal{M}}(\Delta)) \\
\geq \; & \lambda(\mathcal{I}(\Delta')) + \lambda(\mathcal{I}(-\Delta')) + \lambda(\mathcal{M}(\Delta)) \quad = 1
\end{aligned}
$$

a contradiction.$\diamondsuit$

Proof of Proposition 2.5 Obviously, 3−independence implies that two different value vectors cannot be equal, hence the uniqueness of the shadow decision-maker: $\mathcal{M}(0) = \{i(j)\}$.

Now consider another voter, $i \neq i(j)$, and let $\Delta = \mathrm{proj}_{T_y} \nabla_i$. The 3-independence condition implies: $\mathcal{M}(\Delta) = \{i(j), i\}$. By Lemma B.1, y must be 0.5^-−majority stable in the electorate $\{i(j), i\}$. If it were the case that $\lambda_{i(j)} < \lambda_i$, then deviation Δ would be supported by a majority of voters within electorate $\{i(j), i\}$, a contradiction.$\diamondsuit$

Proof of Proposition 2.6 Consider indeed $I = \ell$ and $(\nabla_i)_{i \in \mathcal{I}}$'s that are the vertices of a $(\ell - 1)$−dimensional simplex. Suppose that $\rho \leq 1 - 1/\ell$: coalitions of $\ell - 1$ voters are decisive. We know from Proposition 2.3 that for a plan to be stable, it has to be optimal with respect to a value vector in the intersection of the convex hulls of the vertices of all coalitions of $\ell - 1$ voters, i.e. in the intersection of all $(\ell - 2)$-dimensional facets of the simplex. This intersection is empty.$\diamondsuit$

Proof of Lemma 3.1 An allocation $(x^*, y(a^*)) \in \mathbb{R}^{\ell I} \times \mathcal{Y}$ is Pareto-optimal only if it is a solution of the planner's optimization program:

$$
\begin{aligned}
\max_{(x,a)} \quad & u_1(x_1) \\
\text{s.t.} \quad & \begin{cases} u_i(x_i) = u_i(x_i^*), \forall i \geq 2 \\ g_j(a_j) = 0, \forall j \\ \sum_i (x_i - x_i^*) = \sum_j f_j(a) \end{cases}
\end{aligned}
$$

The first-order conditions of this program mean that there exist $((\alpha_i)_i, (\beta_j)_j, \mu) \in \mathbb{R}_+^{I-1} \times \mathbb{R}_+^J \times \mathbb{R}_+^\ell$ such that:

$$
\left.
\begin{aligned}
\alpha_i D u_i(x_i) - \mu &= 0 \quad \forall i \\
g_j(a_j) &= 0 \quad \forall j \\
\left(\sum_{j'} D_{a_j} f_{j'}(a) \right)^T \mu - \beta_j D g_j(a_j) &= 0 \quad \forall j
\end{aligned}
\right\}
$$

Given that x_i is a solution to the consumer problem, with the right rescaling of the α_i's and β_j's, μ can be identified with the price vector p^*, and $Dg_j(a_j)$ can be identified to the value vector ∇_j.

The two last first-order conditions of the planner's program are equivalent to the first-order conditions of the firm's profit maximization:

$$\max_{a_j} \quad p^* \cdot \sum_{j'} f_{j'}(a_j, a^*_{-j})$$
$$\text{s.t.} \quad g_j(a_j) = 0$$

Perfect internalization happens when actions are optimized with respect to the value vector $\sum_{j'} D_{a_j} f_{j'}(a)^T p.\diamond$

Proof of Proposition 3.1 See Theorem 3 in Crès & Tvede (2013).$\diamond$

Proof of Theorem 3.1 Suppose $d < J$ and consider the image sub-space of the operator Ξ_j (denoted $\text{Im}\Xi_j$), i.e. the sub-space of $\mathbb{R}^{J-1}$ generated by the column vector of $\Xi_j : (D_{a_j} f_{j'}(a)^T p)_{j' \in \mathcal{J}}$. It has a dimension smaller or equal to d; without loss of generality, we assume it has dimension d and take the first d vectors as a basis. Recall that the vector $D_{a_j} f_{j'}(a)^T p$ measures the value of the marginal impact of the action of firm j on the profit of firm j'. These marginal impacts are determined by the exogenously fixed production function. Randomizing over the production function amounts to randomizing over $\text{Im}\Xi_j$, hence it is natural to use the Grassmann approach.

The collection of portfolios $(\theta_i)_{i \in \mathcal{I}}$ indeed compose the J vertices of a spherico-regular $(J-1)$-dimensional simplex, $\mathbb{S}^J$. It is regular since $\|\theta_i - \theta_{i'}\| > 0$ has the same value for all $i \neq i'$; moreover it is spherico-regular since the vertices lie on a sphere centered at the origin.

The Grassmann approach amounts to randomly rotating $\mathbb{S}^J$ and projecting it orthogonally onto a fixed d-dimensional subspace. Without loss of generality, $\mathbb{S}^J$ can be suitably translated so that it becomes centered: the sum of its vertices (the scaled-down market portfolio $(1/J)1_J$, center of gravity under the stakeholder democracy) is translated at zero. Once more without loss of generality, the fixed d-dimensional subspace onto which the rotated simplex is projected can be taken as the first d coordinates of $\mathbb{R}^J$. But the operator Ξ_j is not this orthogonal projection, but a linear (thus affine) transformation of the latter (one can pass from one to the other using the Gram–Schmidt procedure between the standard orthonormal basis and the basis defined by $(D_{a_j} f_{j'}(a)^T p)_{1 \leq j' \leq d}$). The composition of affine transformation being affine, we can directly apply Baryshnikov and Vitale (1994) to our problem, only exploiting the symmetry of the generated distribution.

Under the Grassman approach on production externalities, within every firm j, the point set $(\nabla_{ij})_{i \in \mathcal{J}}$ coincides in distribution with a standard centered Gaussian sample. Therefore the convergence of the min–max of the sample to the min–max of the Gaussian distribution is a consequence of Proposition 2.7.$\diamond$

Proof of Lemma 3.2 Similar to Lemma 3.1, the necessary and sufficient first-order conditions for Pareto optimality mean that there exist $((\alpha_i)_i, \beta, \mu) \in \mathbb{R}^{I-1}_+ \times \mathbb{R}_+ \times \mathbb{R}^\ell_+$ such that:

$$\left. \begin{array}{r} \forall i, \quad \alpha_i Du_i(x_i) - \mu = 0 \\ g(y) = 0 \\ \mu - \beta Dg(y) = 0 \end{array} \right\}$$

Hence the result.$\diamondsuit$

Proof of Proposition 3.2 Suppose $0_\ell \in \bigcap_{\mathcal{M} \in \mathcal{D}^\rho} \angle^+ (z_i)_{i \in \mathcal{M}}$. For all $\mathcal{M} \in \mathcal{D}^\rho$, there is $\mu \in \mathbb{R}_{++}^{|\mathcal{M}|}$ such that $\sum_{i \in \mathcal{M}} \mu_i z_i = 0$. Hence $\sum_{i \in \mathcal{M}} \mu_i \nabla_i = \left(\sum_{i \in \mathcal{M}} \mu_i \bar{\theta}_i \right) p$. Therefore

$$p \in \bigcap_{\mathcal{M} \in \mathcal{D}^\rho} \angle^+ (\nabla_i)_{i \in \mathcal{M}}$$

hence the result.$\diamondsuit$

Proof of Corollary 3.4 Given Lemma 1.3, considering the sign of $U_i(x_i^* + \theta_{ij}^* \Delta y + w_i 1_\ell) - U_i(x_i^*)$ is equivalent to considering the sign of

$$\theta_{ij}^* DU_i(x_i^*) \cdot \Delta y + w_i DU_i(x_i^*) \cdot 1_\ell = DU_i(x_i^*) \cdot 1_\ell \left(\theta_{ij}^* \nabla_i^{\|}(x_i^*) \cdot \Delta y + w_i \right)$$

where $\nabla_i^{\|}(x_i^*)$ stands for the normalized gradient at equilibrium. The corollary results from a direct application of Proposition 2.2, with $\nabla_i = \theta_{ij}^* \nabla_i^{\|}(x_i^*)$.$\diamondsuit$

Proof of Proposition 3.3 See Proposition 31.8 in Magill & Quinzii (1996).$\diamondsuit$

Proof of Corollary 3.5 At an equilibrium that is stable with respect to sidepayment, any proposed direction of (infinitesimal) change Δy is, by construction, orthogonal to the valuation vector with respect to which value is maximized, i.e. $\nabla_j^* \cdot \Delta y = 0$. Therefore any change Δy will be supported by a half space of the set of present value vectors cutting this through its centroid. A direct application of Theorem 2.2 yields that for every j, ∇_j^* is $\rho(\ell - J + 1/\sigma)$−majority stable.$\diamondsuit$

Proof of Proposition 3.4 Let us first note that the gradients, $DU_i(x_i) = \Pi(\gamma_i 1_\ell - x_i)$, and the optimal portfolios given by equation (B.1) are linear functions of the fundamental characteristics of the agents, $\iota = (\gamma, \bar{x})$. Indeed, consider two agents (ι, ι'), for all $t \in [0, 1]$,

$$DU_{t\iota + (1-t)\iota'}(tx + (1-t)x') = t DU_\iota(x) + (1-t) DU_{\iota'}(x')$$

and moreover $\theta_{t\iota + (1-t)\iota'} = t\theta_\iota + (1-t)\theta_{\iota'}$.

The distribution of voting weights on the set $\mathcal{I}$ is $\varphi \lambda_j$ for firm j. Let us suppose that φ is σ−concave over a compact and convex support. Since θ_j is linear, hence 1−concave, $\varphi \lambda_j$ is $\sigma/(\sigma + 1)$−concave over a compact and convex support, as follows from Lemma B.2 below.

Let us now turn toward the induced density $\varphi \lambda_j$ on the support, denoted $\mathcal{N}$, of normalized value vectors. Consider two of them, $\nabla^{\|}$ and $\nabla^{\|\prime} \in \mathcal{N}$. Their pre-images in $\mathcal{I}$, denoted L and L', are linear sub-spaces; e.g. L is the pre-image through gradient DU of a line in $\mathbb{R}^\ell$. For all $t \in [0, 1]$, given the convexity of $\mathcal{I}$, the pre-image, L_t, of $t\nabla_{\|} + (1-t)\nabla_{\|}'$ in $\mathcal{I}$ includes the Minkowski average of L and L', $tL + (1-t)L'$. Hence

$$\int_{L_t} \varphi(\iota)\lambda_j(\iota) d\iota \geq \int_{tL + (1-t)L'} \varphi(\iota)\lambda_j(\iota) d\iota$$

The Prékopa–Borell theorem (see Caplin & Nalebuff, 1991) gives:

$$\int_{tL+(1-t)L'} f\varphi(\iota)\lambda_j(\iota)d\iota \geq \left[t\left(\int_L \varphi(\iota)\lambda_j(\iota)d\iota \right)^\phi + (1-t)\left(\int_L \varphi(\iota)\lambda_j d\iota \right)^\phi \right]^{1/\phi}$$

where $\phi = \sigma/[1 + (\ell + 2)\sigma)]$. Hence the result.$\diamondsuit$

Lemma B.2 *if $\varphi : K \to \mathbb{R}_+$ is σ-concave and $\psi : K \to \mathbb{R}_+$ is τ-concave, then $\varphi \times \psi$ is ν-concave for all*

$$\nu \leq \frac{\sigma\tau}{\sigma + \tau}.$$

Proof of Lemma B.2 See Crès & Tvede (2009).$\diamondsuit$

Proof of Proposition 4.1 Let us disentangle the prior value vector $\tilde{\nabla}_i$ from the posterior one ∇_i when shareholder i aggregates. The Pareto principle could be reformulated as:

$$\tilde{\nabla}_i \cdot \Delta y \geq 0 \text{ and } \nabla_j \cdot \Delta y \geq 0 \; \forall \, j \in \mathcal{J}_i \text{ (with at least one >)} \Rightarrow \nabla_i \cdot \Delta y > 0.$$

Then a straightforward application of Proposition 2.1 yields that there are $\mu_i > 0$ and $(\mu_{ij})_{j \in \mathcal{J}_i}$ with $\mu_{ij} > 0$ such that

$$\nabla_i = \mu_i \tilde{\nabla}_i + \sum_{j \in \mathcal{J}_i} \mu_{ij} \nabla_j.$$

Since the ∇_i's are independent, $0 < \mu_i < 1$; moreover, ultimately $\nabla_i = \tilde{\nabla}_i$, hence the result with coefficients $\nu_{ij} = \frac{\mu_{ij}}{1-\mu_i}$.$\diamondsuit$

Proof of Theorem 4.1 Let $P_{\mathcal{I}}$ be the convex hull of value vectors $(\nabla_i)_{i \in \mathcal{I}}$ and $P_{\mathcal{J}}$ the convex hull of value vectors $(\nabla_j)_{j \in \mathcal{J}}$. Then $P_{\mathcal{I}} = P_{\mathcal{J}}$ according to Propositions 2.1 and 4.1.
  Suppose p is an extreme points of $P_{\mathcal{I}} = P_{\mathcal{J}}$ and let $\mathcal{I}(p) = \{\, i \in \mathcal{I} \mid \nabla_i(U_i, x_i) = p \,\}$ and $\mathcal{J}(p) = \{\, j \in \mathcal{J} \mid \nabla_j(y_j) = p \,\}$. Then $\mathcal{I}(p), \mathcal{J}(p) \neq \emptyset$ by construction. Moreover for every $i \in \mathcal{I}(p)$, $\mathcal{J}_i \subset \mathcal{J}(p)$ according to Proposition 2.1 and for every $j \in \mathcal{J}(p)$, $\mathcal{I}_j \subset \mathcal{I}(p)$ according to Proposition 4.1 because p is an extreme point of $P_{\mathcal{I}} = P_{\mathcal{J}}$. Since $\mathcal{G}(\theta)$ is connected, $\mathcal{I}(p) = \mathcal{I}$ and $\mathcal{J}(p) = \mathcal{J}$.$\diamondsuit$

Proof of Corollary 4.2 A sufficient condition for Pareto optimality is that all consumer gradients be collinear and that production be optimized with respect to this common present value vector. We know from Theorem 4.1 that both conditions hold.$\diamondsuit$

Proof of Corollary 4.3 Given that a_j (superscripts * are abandoned for lightness of notation) is stable with respect to the Pareto principle, Proposition 2.1 implies that $\forall j, \exists$ $\mu_i \in \mathbb{S}_+^{|\mathcal{I}_j|}$ such that $\nabla_j = \sum_{i \in \mathcal{I}_j} \mu_{ji} \nabla_{ij}$.
  One has: $\sum_{i \in \mathcal{I}_j} \mu_{ji} \nabla_{ij} = \sum_{i \in \mathcal{I}_j} \mu_{ji} \Xi_j \theta_i = \Xi_j \sum_{i \in \mathcal{I}_j} \mu_{ji} \theta_i$. Hence $\theta_j = \sum_{i \in \mathcal{I}_j} \mu_{ji} \theta_i$, therefore $\theta_j \in \angle^+(\theta_i)_{i \in \mathcal{I}_j}$.

Now, consider the (implicit) portfolio $\theta_{j'}$ of firm j' and apply it to firm j; this gives the value vector $\nabla_{jj'} = \Xi_j \theta_{j'}$, interpreted by shareholders of firm j as conveying the expertise of board j' on how to run firm j. We assume that in assessing her value vector ∇_{ij}, shareholder i aggregates the $\nabla_{jj'}$'s across every $j' \in \mathcal{J}_i$, abiding by the Pareto principle across firms. Next, Proposition 4.1 implies that $\forall i, \forall j \in \mathcal{J}_i$, $\exists \xi_{ij} \in \mathbb{S}_+^{|\mathcal{J}_i|}$ such that $\nabla_{ij} = \sum_{j' \in \mathcal{J}_i} \xi_{ijj'} \nabla_{jj'}$.

One then has $\sum_{j' \in \mathcal{J}_i} \xi_{ijj'} \nabla_{jj'} = \sum_{j' \in \mathcal{J}_i} \xi_{ijj'} \Xi_j \theta_{j'} = \Xi_j \sum_{j' \in \mathcal{J}_i} \xi_{ijj'} \theta_{j'}$. Therefore $\theta_{ij} = \sum_{j' \in \mathcal{J}_i} \xi_{ijj'} \theta_{j'}$ is the portfolio through which shareholder i assesses the value of decisions in firm j. For reasons of internal consistency of choice at the individual level, these portfolios must be the same for every j. Hence $\xi_{ijj'} = \xi_{ij'}$ for every j. This yields $\theta_i \in \angle^+ (\theta_j)_{j \in \mathcal{J}_i}$. $\Diamond$

Proof of Remark 4.1 Fix $\theta_j = 1_J$ for every j, $q_j = p \cdot f_j(a)$ and choose

$$a_j = \arg\max \left\{ \sum_{j'} p \cdot f_{j'}(a'_j, a_{-j}) \mid a'_j \in \mathcal{A}_j \right\}$$

i.e. all firms maximize the joint profit. The existence of a market equilibrium (for fixed actions) (p^*, x^*) follows from the standard Walrasian analysis (see, e.g., Balasko, 2011).

Fix $\theta_i = t_i 1_J$ for every i, with $\sum_i t_i = 1$ and $t_i > 0$. Then in every firm j, all consumers have collinear value vectors: $\nabla_{ij} = t_i \Xi_j 1_J$, and moreover they all agree on the choice of a_j, so $(\nabla_j(y_j))_{j \in \mathcal{J}}$ is Pareto-stable across shareholders.

Reciprocally, since all firms optimize production according to the market portfolio, and so do the shareholders, $(\nabla_i(U_i, x_i))_{i \in \mathcal{I}}$ are Pareto-stable across firms. $\Diamond$

Proof of Remark 4.2 Fix a present value vector $\nabla \in \mathbb{S}^\ell$. Define $y_j^* = \arg\max\{ \nabla \cdot y_j \mid y_j \in \mathcal{Y}_j \}$ for every j, and consequently a^*. Consider a market equilibrium (q^*, x^*, y^*) for $\bar{U}$— existence of such an equilibrium is standard (see, e.g., Theorem 10.5 in Magill & Quinzii 1996). Define $\pi_i^* = \pi(x_i^*, \nabla)$. Then $(q^*, \pi^* \cdot \bar{u}, \theta^*, x^*, y^*)$ is a reciprocal aggregation equilibrium. $\Diamond$

Proof of Lemma 4.1 As for Lemma 1.2, the first-order conditions of the optimization problem of consumer i yield: $\exists \lambda_i \in \mathbb{R}_+$ such that $DU_i(x_i) = \Pi_i(\gamma_i 1_\ell - x_i) = \lambda_i p$.

Hence $x_i = \gamma_i 1_\ell - \lambda_i \Pi_i^{-1} p$. Adding individual consumptions: $\sum_k x_k = \Gamma 1_\ell - \left(\sum_{k \in \mathcal{I}} \lambda_k \Pi_k^{-1} \right) p = \Omega$, where the diagonal matrix $\left(\sum_{k \in \mathcal{I}} \lambda_k \Pi_k^{-1} \right)$ is invertible and therefore for every i

$$x_i = \gamma_i 1_\ell - V_i (\Gamma 1_\ell - \Omega) \text{ where } V_i = \lambda_i \Pi_i^{-1} \left(\sum_{k \in \mathcal{I}} \lambda_k \Pi_k^{-1} \right)^{-1};$$

V_i is a diagonal matrix whose generic element is $v_i^s = (\lambda_i / \pi_i^s) / (\sum_{k \in \mathcal{I}} \lambda_k / \pi_k^s)$; therefore $v_i = (v_i^1, \ldots, v_i^\ell) \in \mathbb{S}_+^\ell$ is a probability vector.

The normalization of the price vector p and the $(I - 1)$ independent budget constraints give I equations that allow us to determine the values of $(\lambda_k)_{k \in \mathcal{I}}$. It is not necessary to compute them.

Let us show that the matrix $D_{(\hat{\pi}_i, \gamma_i)} x_i$ has complete rank. First of all, its $(\ell - 1)$ first column vectors:

$$\frac{dx_i}{d\pi_i^s} = -\frac{dV_i}{d\pi_i^s}(\Gamma 1_\ell - \Omega)$$

form a diagonal, as their coordinates are all zero, except the s-th, with value $\frac{dv_i^s}{d\pi_i^s}(\Gamma-\Omega^s) \neq$ 0. and its ℓ-th column vector

$$\frac{dx_i}{d\gamma_i} = 1_\ell - V_i 1_\ell - \frac{dV_i}{d\gamma_i}(\Gamma 1_\ell - \Omega)$$

has a ℓ-th coordinate which is non-zero generically. $\Diamond$

References

Affentranger, F. & Schneider, R. (1992), Random Projection of Regular Simplices, *Discrete Computational Geometry,* 11: 141–147.

Ambrus, A. & Rozen, K. (2008), Rationalizing Choice with Multi-Self Models, *Cowles Foundation Discussion Paper,* 1670.

Arrow, K.J. (1951), *Social Choice and Individual Values,* New York: Wiley.

Arrow, K.J. (1953), Le rôle des valeurs boursières pour la répartition la meilleure des risques, *Fondements et applications de la théorie du risque en économétrie,* Paris: CNRS.

Arrow, K.J. (1969), The Organization of Economic Activity: Issues Pertinent to Market versus Non-market Analysis, in *The Analysis and Evaluation of Public Expenditure: The PPBS System,* Washington, DC: Congress Joint Economic Committee, pp. 47–64.

Arrow, K. (1984), *Collected Papers of Kenneth J. Arrow,* Volume 1: *Social Choice and Justice,* Cambridge, MA: Belknap Press.

Arrow, K.J. & Debreu, G. (1954), Existence of an Equilibrium for a Competitive Economy, *Econometrica,* 22(3): 265–290.

Balasko, Y. (1988), *Foundations of the Theory of General Equilibrium,* Boston: Academic Press.

Balasko, Y. (1990), Equivariant General Equilibrium Theory, *Journal of Economic Theory,* 52: 18–44.

Balasko, Y. (2011), *General Equilibrium Theory of Value,* Princeton: Princeton University Press.

Balasko, Y. & Crès, H. (1997), Condorcet Cycles and Super-Majority Rules, *Journal of Economic Theory,* 70: 437–470.

Balasko, Y. & Crès, H. (1998), Condorcet Cycles in Bipartite Populations, *Economic Theory,* 12: 313–334.

Baryshnikov, Y.M. & Vitale, R.A. (1994), Regular Simplices and Gaussian Samples, *Discrete Computational Geometry,* 7: 219–226.

Becker, G.S. (1976), *The Economic Approach to Human Behavior,* Chicago: University of Chicago Press.

Becker, G.S. (1996), *Accounting For Tastes,* Cambridge, MA: Harvard University Press.

Bejan, C. (2008), The Objective of a Privately Owned Firm under Imperfect Competition, *Economic Theory,* 37(1): 99–118.

Benhabib, J., Bisin, A. & Jackson, M.O. (eds.) (2011), *The Handbook of Social Economics,* Amsterdam: North Holland.

Benninga, S. & Muller, E. (1979), Majority Choice and the Objective Function of the Firm under Uncertainty, *Bell Journal of Economics,* Fall: 670–682.

Bernoulli, D. (1738), Specimen theoriae novae de mensura sortis, *Mémoires de l'Académie impériale des sciences de St. Pétersbourg,* 5: 175–192.

Bisin, A. & Gottardi, P. (2006), Efficient Competitive Equilibria with Adverse Selection, *Journal of Political Economy,* 114: 485–516.

Bisin, A. & Verdier, T. (2001), The Economics of Cultural Transmission and the Dynamics of Preferences, *Journal of Economic Theory,* 97: 298–319.

Black, D. (1948), On the Rationale of Group Decision-making, *Journal of Political Economy,* 56: 23–34.

Black, D. (1958), *The Theory of Committees and Elections.* Cambridge: Cambridge University Press.

Bolton, P., Tao, L., Ravina, E. & Rosenthal, H. (2019), Investor Ideology, *ECGI Working Paper Series in Finance,* No. 557/2018.

Bovens, L. (1992), Sour Grapes and Character Planning, *Journal of Philosophy,* 89(2): 57–78.

Bowles, S. (1998), Endogenous Preferences: The Cultural Consequences of Markets and Other Economic Institutions, *Journal of Economic Literature,* 36(1): 75–111.

Brehm, J. (1956), Post-decision Changes in Desirability of Alternatives, *Journal of Abnormal and Social Psychology,* 52(3): 384–389.

Breiger, R. (1974), The Duality of Persons and Groups, *Social Forces,* 53(2): 181–190.

Britz, V., Herings, J.J. & Predtetchinski, A. (2013), A Bargaining Theory of the Firm, *Economic Theory,* 54: 45–75.

Burns, T. (1961), Micropolitics: Mechanisms of Organizational Change, *Administrative Science Quarterly,* 6: 257–281.

Burns, T. and Stalker, G. M. (1961), *The Management of Innovation,* London: Tavistock.

Caplin, A. & Nalebuff, B. (1988), On the 64%-majority Rule, *Econometrica,* 56:(4), 787–814.

Caplin, A. & Nalebuff, B. (1991), Aggregation and Social Choice: A Mean Voter Theorem, *Econometrica,* 59: 1–23.

Champsaur, P. (1976), Symmetry and Continuity Properties of Lindahl Equilibria, *Journal of Mathematical Economy,* 3: 19–36.

Chiappori, P.-A. & Ekeland, I. (2006), The Microeconomics of Group Behavior: General Characterization, *Journal of Economic Theory,* 130: 1–26.

Coase, R.H. (1960), The Problem of Social Cost, *Journal of Law and Economics,* 3: 1–44.

Condorcet, M.J. (1785), *Essai sur l'application de l'analyse à la probabilité des décisions rendues à la pluralité des voix,* Paris.

Crès, H. (1996), Symmetric Smooth Consumption Externalities, *Journal of Economic Theory,* 69: 334–366.

Crès, H. (2001), Aggregation of Coarse Preferences, *Social Choice and Welfare,* 18: 507–525.

Crès, H. (2006), A Geometric Study of Shareholders' Voting in Incomplete Markets: Multivariate Median and Mean Shareholder Theorems, *Social Choice and Welfare,* 27: 377–406.

Crès, H. (2018), L'approche economique des décisions d'assemblées, in Rozenberg, O. & Thiers, E. (eds.), *Traité d'études parlementaires,* Paris: Bruylant, pp. 501–538.

Crès, H. & Rossi, I. (2000), Symmetry Breakings in Malinvaud's Model with Individual Risks, *Journal of Mathematical Economics,* 33: 239–269.

Crès, H. & Tvede, M. (2009), Production in Incomplete Markets: Expectations Matter for Political Stability, *Journal of Mathematical Economics,* 45: 212–222.

Crès, H. & Tvede, M. (2013), Production Externalities: Internalization by Voting, *Economic Theory,* 53: 403–424.

Crès, H. & Tvede, M. (2018), Regulation of Trades Based on Differences in Beliefs, *European Economic Review,* 101: 133–141.

Crès, H. & Tvede, M. (2020), Corporate Self-Regulation of Imperfect Competition, working paper.

Crès, H. & Ünver, U. (2010), Ideology and Existence of 50%-majority Equilibria in Multi-dimensional Spatial Voting Models, *Journal of Theoretical Politics* 22: 431–444.

Crès, H., Ghiglino, C. & Tvede, M. (1997), Externalities, Internalization and Fluctuations, *International Economic Review,* 38: 465–477.

Crès, H., Gilboa, I. & Vieille, N. (2011), Aggregation of Multiple Prior Opinions, *Journal of Economic Theory*, 146: 2563–2582.

Debreu, G. (1959), *The Theory of Value*. New Haven: Yale University Press, Cowles Foundation Monographs Series.

DeGroot, M.H. (1974), Reaching a Consensus, *Journal of the American Statistical Association*, 69: 118–121.

DeMarzo, P. (1993), Majority Voting and Corporate Control: The Rule of the Dominant Shareholder, *Review of Economic Studies*, 60: 713–734.

DeMeyer, F. & Plott, C.R. (1970), The Probability of a Cyclical Majority, *Econometrica*, 38: 345–354.

Dierker, E. & Grodal, B. (1999), The Price Normalization Problem in Imperfect Competition and the Objective of the Firm, *Economic Theory*, 14(2): 257–284.

Dietrich, F. & List, C. (2011), A Model of Non-informational Preference Change, *Journal of Theoretical Politics*, 23(2): 145–164.

Dixit, A.K. & Nalebuff, B.J. (1993), *Thinking Strategically: The Competitive Edge in Business, Politics, and Everyday Life*, New York: W.W. Norton.

Drèze, J. (1974), Investment under Private Ownership: Optimality, Equilibrium and Stability, in J. Drèze (ed.), *Allocation under Uncertainty: Equilibrium and Optimality*, New York: Wiley.

Drèze, J. (1985), (Uncertainty and) the Firm in General Equilibrium Theory, in J. Drèze (ed.), *Essays on Economic Decisions under Uncertainty*, New York, NY: Wiley.

Dryzek, J. & List, C. (2003), Social Choice Theory and Deliberative Democracy: A Reconciliation, *British Journal of Political Science*, 33: 1–28.

Duffie, D. (2014), Challenges to a Policy Treatment of Speculative Trading Motivated by Differences in Beliefs, *Journal of Legal Studies*, 43: 173–182.

Dworkin, G. (1988), *The Theory and Practice of Autonomy*, Cambridge: Cambridge University Press.

Elster, J. (1983), *Sour Grapes: Studies in the Subversion of Rationality*, Cambridge: Cambridge University Press.

Fayol, H. (1919), *General and Industrial Management*, English translation, 1949, London: Pitman.

de Finetti, B. (1937), La prévision: ses lois logiques, ses sources subjectives, *Annales de l'Institut Henri Poincaré*, 7: 1–68.

Fisher, I. (1930), *The Theory of Interest*. New York: Macmillan.

Friedman, M. (1962), *Capitalism and Freedom*, Chicago: University of Chicago Press.

Friedman, M. (1970), The Social Responsibility of Business Is to Increase Its Profits. *New York Times Magazine*, Sept. 13.

Gabszewicz, J. & Vial, J.-P. (1972), Oligopoly à la Cournot in a General Equilibrium Analysis, *Journal of Economic Theory*, 4: 381–400.

Gayer, G., Gilboa, I., Samuelson, L. & Schmeidler, D. (2014), Pareto Efficiency with Different Beliefs, *Journal of Legal Studies*, 43: 151–172.

Gehrlein, W.V. & Fishburn, P.C. (1976), The Probability of the Paradox of Voting: A Computable Solution, *Journal of Economic Theory* 13: 14–25.

Gevers, L. (1974), Competitive Equilibrium of the Stock Exchange and Pareto Efficiency, in J. Drèze (ed.), *Allocation under Uncertainty: Equilibrium and Optimality*, New York: Wiley, pp. 000–000.

Gilboa, I. (2009), *Theory of Decision under Uncertainty*, Cambridge: Cambridge University Press.

Gilboa, I. (2011), *Making Better Decisions*, New York: John Wiley & Sons.

Gilboa, I. & Schmeidler, D. (1995), Case Based Decision Theory, *Quarterly Journal of Economics,* 110: 605–639.

Gilboa, I., Samuelson, L. & Schmeidler, D. (2014), No-Betting-Pareto Dominance, *Econometrica,* 82: 1405–1442.

Goldman, A. (1972), Toward a Theory of Social Power, *Philosophical Studies,* 23: 221–268.

Grandmont, J.-M. (1978), Intermediate Preferences and Majority-Rule, *Econometrica,* 46: 317–330.

Greenberg, J. (1979), Consistent Majority Rules over Compact Sets of Alternatives, *Econometrica,* 47: 627–636.

Grossman, S.J. & Hart, O. (1979), A Theory of Competitive Equilibrium in Stock Market Economies, *Econometrica,* 47: 293–330.

Guilbaud, G.T. (1952), Les théories de l'intérêt général et le problème logique de l'agrégation, *Économie appliquée,* 5: 501–584.

Habermas, J. (1984), *The Theory of Communicative Action,* Boston: Beacon Press.

Hammond, P. (1976), Changing Tastes and Coherent Dynamic Choice, *Review of Economic Studies,* 43: 159–173.

Hansen, R.G. & Lott, J.R. (1996), Externalities and Corporate Objectives in a World with Diversified Shareholder/Consumers, *Journal of Financial and Quantitative Analysis,* 31(1): 43–68.

Harsanyi, J.C. (1955), Cardinal Welfare, Individualistic Ethics, and Interpersonal Comparison of Utility, *Journal of Political Economy,* 63: 309–321.

Hirschman, A.O. (1970), *Exit, Voice and Loyalty,* Cambridge, MA: Harvard University Press.

Hirshleifer, D. & Shumway, T. (2003), Good Day Sunshine: Stock Returns and the Weather, *Journal of Finance,* 58(3): 1009–1032.

Hotelling, H. (1929), Stability in Competition, *Economic Journal,* 39(153): 41–57.

Hylland, A. & R. Zeckhauser, R. (1979), The Impossibility of Bayesian Group Decision Making with Separate Aggregation of Beliefs and Values, *Econometrica,* 6: 1321–1336.

Izuma, K., Matsumoto, M., Murayama, K., Samejima, K., Sadato, N. & Matsumoto, K. (2010), Neural Correlates of Cognitive Dissonance and Choice-Induced Preference Change, *Proceedings of the National Academy of Sciences,* 107(51): 22014–22019.

Jackson, M.O. (2008), *Social and Economic Networks,* Princeton: Princeton University Press.

Kahn, J.-F. (1995), *La pensée unique,* Paris: Fayard.

Kahneman, D. & Tversky, A. (1979), Prospect Theory: An Analysis of Decision under Risk, *Econometrica,* 47(2): 263–292.

Kahneman, D., Knetsch, J.L. & Thaler, R.H. (1991). Anomalies: The Endowment Effect, Loss Aversion, and Status Quo Bias. *Journal of Economic Perspectives,* 5(1): 193–206.

Kelsey, D. & Milne, F. (1996), The Existence of Equilibrium in Incomplete Markets and the Objective of the Firm, *Journal of Mathematical Economics,* 25: 229–245.

Knight, J. & Johnson, J. (1994), Aggregation and Deliberation: On the Possibility of Democratic Legitimacy, *Political Theory,* 22: 277–296.

Kornhauser, L.A. & Sager, L.G. (1986), Unpacking the Court, *The Yale Law Journal,* 96: 82–117.

Köszegi, B. & Rabin, M. (2006), A Model of Reference-Dependent Preferences, *Quarterly Journal of Economics,* 121(4): 1133–1165.

Kramer, G.H. (1972), Sophisticated Voting over Multidimensional Choice Spaces, *Journal of Mathematical Sociology,* 2: 165–180.

Kramer, G.H. (1973), On a Class of Equilibrium Conditions for Majority Rule, *Econometrica*, 41: 285–297.

Laffont, J.J. & Martimort, D. (2002), *The Theory of Incentives*, Princeton: Princeton University Press.

Lancaster, K.J. (1966a), Change and Innovation in the Technology of Consumption, *American Economic Review [P&P]*, 56: 14–23.

Lancaster, K.J. (1966b), A New Approach to Consumer Theory, *Journal of Political Economy*, 74: 132–157.

Latour, B. (2005), *Reassembling the Social: An Introduction to Actor-Network Theory*, Oxford: Oxford University Press.

Lindahl, E. (1958), Just Taxation: A Positive Solution, in Musgrave, R. & Peacock, A. (eds.), *Classics in the Theory of Public Finance*, London: Macmillan, pp. 98–123.

List, C. & Pettit, P. (2002), Aggregating Sets of Judgments: An Impossibility Result, *Economics and Philosophy*, 18: 89–110.

List, C. & Pettit, P. (2011), *Group Agency*, Oxford: Oxford University Press.

List C. & Spiekermann, K. (2013), Methodological Individualism and Holism in Political Science: A Reconciliation, *American Political Science Review*, 107(4): 629–643.

McGann, A. (2006), *The Logic of Democracy*, Ann Arbor: University of Michigan Press.

McKelvey, R.D. (1976), Intransitivities in Multidimensional Voting Models and Some Implications for Agenda Control, *Journal of Economic Theory*, 12: 472–482.

McKenzie, L. (1954), On Equilibrium in Graham's Model of World Trade and Other Competitive Systems, *Econometrica*, 22(2): 147–161.

Magill, M. & Quinzii, M. (1996), *Theory of Incomplete Markets*, Cambridge, MA: MIT Press.

Malinvaud, E. (1972), The Allocation of Individual Risks in Large Markets, *Journal of Economic Theory*, 4: 312–328.

Malinvaud, E. (1973), Markets for an Exchange Economy with Individual Risks, *Econometrica*, 41: 383–410.

March, J.G. (1962), The Business Firm as a Political Coalition, *Journal of Politics*, 24: 662–678.

March, J.G. (1999), *The Pursuit of Organizational Intelligence*. Malden, MA: Blackwell.

Mas-Colell, A. (1985), *The Theory of General Economic Equilibrium*, Cambridge: Cambridge University Press.

May, K.O. (1952), A Set of Independent Necessary and Sufficient Conditions for Simple Majority Decisions, *Econometrica*, 20(4): 680–684.

Miller, D. (1992), Deliberative Democracy and Social Choice, *Political Studies*, 40: 54–67.

Mongin, P. (1995), Consistent Bayesian Aggregation, *Journal of Economic Theory*, 66: 313–351.

Mongin, P. (1997), Spurious Unanimity and the Pareto Principle, *Université de Cergy-Pontoise Working Paper*.

Mongin, P. (2008), Factoring Out the Impossibility of Logical Aggregation, *Journal of Economic Theory*, 141: 100–113.

Mongin, P. (2012), The Doctrinal Paradox, the Discursive Dilemma, and Logical Aggregation Theory, *Theory and Decision*, 73: 315–355.

Morgan, G. (2006), *Images of Organization*. Thousand Oaks, CA: Sage Publications.

Nehring, K. (2005), The (Im)possibility of a Paretian Rational, working paper.

Nehring, K., Pivato, M., & Puppe, C. (2016), Unanimity Overruled: Majority Voting and the Burden of History, *Journal of Theoretical Politics*, 28: 552–597.

Nelson, P. (1970), Information and Consumer Behavior, *Journal of Political Economy* 78(2): 311–329.

von Neumann, J. & Morgenstern, O. (1944), *Theory of Games and Economic Behavior*, Princeton: Princeton University Press.

Nussbaum, M.C. (2003), Capabilities as Fundamental Entitlements: Sen and Social Justice, *Feminist Economics*, 9(2/3): 33–59.

Nussbaum, M.C. (2004), Promoting Women's Capabilities, in *Global Tensions*, New York: Routledge.

Ouchi, W. & Wilkins, A. (1985), Organizational Culture, *Annual Review of Sociology*, 11: 457–483.

Parsons, T. (1951), *The Social System*, New York: The Free Press.

Pettit, P. (1993), *The Common Mind: An Essay on Psychology, Society and Politics*, Oxford: Oxford University Press.

Plott, C.R. (1967), A Notion of Equilibrium and Its Possibility under the Majority Rule, *American Economic Review*, 57: 787–806.

Pollack, R.A. (1978), Endogenous Tastes in Demand and Welfare Analysis, *American Economic Review*, 68(2): 374–379.

Rockafellar, T. (1970), *Convex Analysis*, Princeton: Princeton University Press.

Rogowski, R. & Linzer, D. (2008a), Electoral Institutions and Real Prices Around the World, 1972 to 2000, *Journal of Politics*, 70.

Rogowski, R., Chang, E. & Kayser, M. (2008b), Electoral Systems and Real Prices: Panel Evidence for the OECD Countries, 1970–2000, *British Journal of Political Science*, 38(4): 739–751.

Roth, A.E., Sönmez, T. & Ünver, M.U. (2004). Kidney Exchange. *Quarterly Journal of Economics*, 119(2): 457–488.

Rozen, K. (2010), Foundations of Intrinsic Habit Formation, *Econometrica*, 78(4): 1341–1373.

Sadanand, A.B., Williamson, J.M. (1991), Equilibrium in a Stock Market Economy with Shareholder Voting. *International Economic Review*, 32: 1–35.

Samuelson, P.A. (1954), The Pure Theory of Public Expenditure, *Review of Economics and Statistics*, 36(4): 387–89.

Sandelands, L.E. and Stablein, R.E. (1987), The Concept of Organization Mind, *Research in the Sociology of Organizations*, 5. Greenwich, CT: JAI Press.

Savage, L.J. (1954), *The Foundations of Statistics*, New York: John Wiley & Sons.

Schneider, R. (2004), Discrete Aspects of Stochastic Geometry, in J.E. Goodman and J. O'Rourke (eds.), *Handbook of Discrete and Computational Geometry*, 2nd ed., Boca Raton: Chapman & Hall/CRC, pp. 255–278.

Sen, A.K. (1970), *Collective Choice and Social Welfare*, Amsterdam: North Holland.

Sen, A.K. (1985), *Commodities and Capabilities*, Oxford: Oxford University Press.

Sen, A.K. (1999), *Development As Freedom*, New York: Knopf.

Sharot, T., Velasquez, C.M. & Dolan, R.J. (2010). Do Decisions Shape Preference? Evidence from Blind Choice. *Psychological Science*, 21(9): 1231–1235.

Simmel, G. (1955), *Conflict and the Web of Group-Affiliations*, New York: Free Press.

Simpson, P.B. (1969), On Defining Areas of Voter Choice, *Quarterly Journal of Economics*, 83: 478–490.

Steedman, I. & Krause, U. (1985), Goethe's Faust, Arrow's Impossibility Theorem and the Individual Decision-Taker, in Elster, J. (ed.), *The Multiple Self*, Cambridge: Cambridge University Press.

Stigler, G.J. & Becker, G.S. (1977), De gustibus non est disputandum, *American Economic Review*, 67(2): 76–90.

Taylor, F.W. (1911), *The Principles of Scientific Management*, New York: Harper.

Thaler, R.H. & Sunstein, C.R. (2008), *Nudge: Improving Decisions about Health, Wealth, and Happiness,* Harmondsworth: Penguin.

Tiebout, C. (1956), A Pure Theory of Local Expenditures, *Journal of Political Economy,* 64(5): 416–424.

Tirole, J. (1988), *The Theory of Industrial Organization,* Cambridge, MA: MIT Press.

Tullock, G. (1967), The General Irrelevance of the General Impossibility Theorem, *Quarterly Journal of Economics,* 81(2): 256–270.

Tullock, G. (1981), Why So Much Stability? *Public Choice,* 37: 189–205.

Tvede, M., & Crès, H. (2005), Voting in Assemblies of Shareholders and Incomplete Markets, *Economic Theory,* 26: 887–906.

Walras, L. (1874), *Éléments d'économie politique pure,* Lausanne: L. Corbaz & Cie.

Walsh, J.P. & Ungson, G.R. (1991), Organizational Memory, *Academy of Management Review,* 16: 57–91.

Weber, M. (1924), *The Theory of Social and Economic Organization.* English translation, 1947, Glencoe, Il: Free.

von Weizsäcker, C.C. (1971), Notes on Endogenous Change of Tastes, *Journal of Economic Theory,* 3(4): 345–371.

von Weizsäcker, C.C. (2013), Freedom, Wealth and Adaptive Preferences, *Max-Planck-Institute Working Paper.*

Index

Note: Figures are indicated by an italic *f* following the page number.